Conversations with Will D. Campbell

Literary Conversations Series
Monika Gehlawat
General Editor

Conversations with Will D. Campbell

Edited by Tom Royals

University Press of Mississippi / *Jackson*

www.upress.state.ms.us

The University Press of Mississippi is a member of
the Association of American University Presses.

First printing 2018

∞

Library of Congress Cataloging-in-Publication Data

Names: Campbell, Will D., interviewee. | Royals, Tom, 1938– editor.
Title: Conversations with Will D. Campbell / edited by Tom Royals.
Description: Jackson : University Press of Mississippi, [2018] | Series:
    Literary conversations series | Includes bibliographical references and
    index. |
Identifiers: LCCN 2017054848 (print) | LCCN 2018000310 (ebook) | ISBN
    9781496814968 (epub single) | ISBN 9781496814975 (epub institutional) |
    ISBN 9781496814982 (pdf single) | ISBN 9781496814999 (pdf
institutional) | ISBN 9781496814951 (hardcover) | ISBN 9781496818140
(pbk.)
Subjects: LCSH: Campbell, Will D.—Interviews. | Baptists—Southern
    States—Clergy—Interviews. | Authors, American—20th century—Interviews.
Classification: LCC PS3553.A488 (ebook) | LCC PS3553.A488 Z46 2018 (print) |
    DDC 813/.54 [B] —dc23
LC record available at https://lccn.loc.gov/2017054848

British Library Cataloging-in-Publication Data available

Books by Will Campbell

Autobiography

Brother to a Dragonfly. Seabury Press, 1977. Republished, New York: Bloomsbury Press, 2000.

Crashing the Idols: The Vocation of Will D. Campbell. Eugene, OR: Wipf and Stock Publishers, 2010.

Forty Acres and a Goat. Perennial Library, 1986. Republished, Oxford, MS: Jefferson Press, 2002.

Fiction

Cecelia's Sin. Macon, GA: Mercer University Press, 1983.

The Convention: A Parable. Atlanta, GA: Peachtree Publishers, 1988.

The Glad River. New York: Holt, Rinehart and Winston, 1982.

Juvenile Fiction

Bluebirds Always Come on Sunday. Franklin, TN: Providence House Publishing, 1997.

Chester and Chun Ling. Nashville, TN: Adington Press, 1989.

The Pear Tree That Bloomed in the Fall. Franklin, TN: Providence House Publishing, 1996.

Shugah and Doops. Franklin, TN: Providence House Publishing, 1997.

Nonfiction

And Also with You: Duncan Gray and the American Dilemma. Franklin, TN: Providence House Publishing, 1997.

And the Criminals with Him: Essays in Honor of Will D. Campbell and All the Reconciled. Ed. with Richard C. Goode. Eugene, OR: Wipf and Stock Publishers, 2012.

Covenant: Faces, Voices, Places. Atlanta, GA: Peachtree Publishers, 1989.

God on Earth: The Lord's Prayer for Our Time. New York: Crossroads Publishing, 1984.

Providence. Atlanta, GA: Longstreet Press, 1992. Reprint 2002.

Race and the Renewal of the Church. Philadelphia: Westminster Press, 1962.

Robert G. Clark's Journey to the House. Jackson: University Press of Mississippi, 2003.

Soul among Lions: Musings of a Bootleg Preacher. Louisville, KY: Westminster John Knox Press, 1999.

The Stem of Jesse: The Costs of Community at a 1960s Southern School. Macon, GA: Mercer University Press, 1995. Reprint 2002.

Up to Our Steeples in Politics. New York: Paulist Press, 1970. Republished, Eugene: Wipf and Stock Publishers, 2005.

Writings on Reconciliation and Resistance. Eugene, OR: Wipf and Stock Publishers, 2010.

"And the Criminals with Him . . ." Lk 23:33; A First-Person Book about Prisons. New York: Paulist Press, 1973.

Contents

Introduction

This book explores the life and works of the late Will Davis Campbell, a Baptist minister recognized for his work in the civil rights movement in America in the 1950s and '60s. Will was born to a Mississippi, subsistence-farming family in 1924 and became an ordained minister when he was barely seventeen years of age. A skilled and courageous writer and preacher, he published numerous books and participated as a peacemaker in most of the civil rights confrontations in the South. Throughout his career, Campbell drew attention for criticizing the institutional churches and supporting women's rights, gay rights, school desegregation, and Vietnam protesters. Conservatives accused him of beings too liberal because of his views on integration, and liberals found fault with him because he believed segregationists were equal in the eyes of God.

After Campbell graduated from East Fork High School in Amite County, Mississippi, the East Fork Baptist Church ordained him. He then studied the ministry at Louisiana College for two years before joining the US Army and serving three years in Southeast Asia as a hospital technician. Upon his discharge Sergeant Campbell married Brenda Fisher until "death did them part." While in the military, Will read Howard Fast's novel *Freedom Road.* That book described the mistreatment of poor black and white people during Reconstruction. Will saw his family reflected in the characters of the novel. That experience changed him greatly. He vowed to dedicate his life and ministry to preaching reconciliation and grace. If people accepted reconciliation, grace, and the teachings of Jesus, they would be kinder to each other, he hoped.

Upon graduation from Wake Forest College with a degree in English literature, he studied at Tulane for one year. In 1952 Will graduated from Yale University with a BA in ministerial studies. After preaching at a small church for two years, he departed from pulpits and steeples (institutional churches) for good. He then served as religious director at University of Mississippi from 1954 to 1956 when he resigned because of threats and pressure from the chancellor about his views regarding integration. The

National Council of Churches (NCC) in New York hired him as a race relations consultant in the southern United States. He got to know and worked with Rev. Martin Luther King, John Lewis, and Andrew Young. He tried to work with the Klan as well in an effort to prevent violence.

Once a young man came into Will's office and demanded, "Just who the hell are you to march with Reverend King and at the same time meet with the Klan?" Will frequently employed humor to deal with people. "Well," he drawled, "I am not at the top of any who's who list at this time. However, like most of us, I do have a name. Would that help"? The young man answered that his name was Kris Kristofferson and that he was going to become a major songwriter. Will, like most everybody in Nashville, played the guitar and wrote a song or two. He told Kris that he was also going to be a great songwriter. The two visited over time and eventually became longtime friends. Campbell and Kristofferson each believed he had important messages to deliver through his works. The fact that much of what each one said went unheeded never caused Campbell to stop preaching and teaching just as Kristofferson never thought of giving up songwriting and singing.

Will Davis Campbell was a prolific writer who published seventeen books in addition to articles in well-known journals and magazines. In his first book, *Race and Renewal of the Church*, published in 1962, he introduced his theories of grace and reconciliation and, as he saw it, the failure of the institutional churches to follow the dictates of scripture. *Brother to a Dragonfly* was a National Book Award finalist and *Time* magazine listed it as one of the ten best books of the 1970s.

Dr. Orley Caudill conducted a comprehensive oral history of Campbell in 1976. Dr. Caudill wrote that Will's life was different from that of most people. Dr. Caudill believed that Will's own statements verified the foregoing conclusions. Caudill says Campbell admitted perceptions of universal experiences in his ministry, mostly outside of the institutional church. Dr. Caudill referred to Will's separation from institutional churches and becoming a preacher without a church. Will did not attend other churches, but worshipped with his own flock at his cabin in Mount Juliet, Tennessee. He was mindful of Matthew 18:20, and 1 Corinthians 5:4 of the King James Bible. The Book of Matthew proclaims "when two or three are gathered together in my name, there am I in the midst of them." Campbell told Dr. Caudill he did not condemn individuals, only institutions.

In 1992 Paul Prather interviewed Will for the *Herald-Leader* newspaper in Lexington, Kentucky, where Campbell spoke and autographed his new book, *Providence*. Their conversation revealed that liberals sent Campbell hate mail for saying KKK members and other racists were as deserving of Christian love as were blacks and liberal whites. Campbell pointed out the dangers of "religiosity" as opposed to genuine dedication to the scriptures. He urged viewing the Bible as a book about "who God is" rather than as a "handbook of rules and regulations." Some scholars compared him to a saint. Others, who were not so kind, called him a renegade bootleg preacher. Will did not want anyone to call him Minister nor Reverend. He preferred Preacher Will, Will, or Brother Will, to those who knew him well.

In his July 2003 interview with Benjamin Houston at Mount Vernon, near Nashville, Will recalls the Nashville lunch counter sit-ins and the violent reactions of the community to the demonstrations. Houston was interviewing Will on behalf of the *Journal of Southern Religion*, published at Florida State University. Will describes months of arrests and filling the jails with protesters, seeing students jerked off the stools, women yanked by their hair, spitting on the protesters, striking, and other abuse of the protestors. Meanwhile at Vanderbilt University, Jim Lawson, a young ministerial student, resigned under pressure from the ministerial school for being a leader in the demonstrations. Nevertheless, the university then expelled him.

The National Council of Churches (NCC) employed him to go wherever there was racial unrest and to work in the background. In 1955 the Campbell family, made up of Will, his wife Brenda, and three children, moved to Nashville to be centrally located in the South and to avoid danger in Mississippi. Because the family had little money, they settled in a modest neighborhood in Nashville. Musicians and writers who were seeking fame in the country music business also inhabited this neighborhood. Later Will was to become friends with many of them.

Seven years of employment as a field director with the National Council of Churches (1956–1963) was challenging for Will because of increased activity in the movement. He was at the Nashville sit-ins from February 13 to May 10, 1960. In 1963, Will was in Birmingham for a year. He was in Little Rock, Arkansas, for almost a year.

There is a photograph of him on the walkway outside the door of the Lorraine Motel in Memphis, where a gunman had assassinated Dr. King within the hour. The police had not yet secured the crime scene. Blood remained on the floor. Will had rushed there when he heard the news of King's death.

He was the only white person who attended the organizational meetings of the Southern Christian Leadership Conference in Atlanta and New Orleans. Some scholars referred to Will as the conscience of the South and compared him to the prophets Jeremiah and Hosea. Charles Marsh interviewed Will in July of 1993 and compared Will to Karl Barth (1886–1968) who has been called the greatest Protestant theologian of the twentieth century. Marsh cited Will's "strong understanding of grace" in his interview preserved at the University of Virginia's Project on Lived Theology. Marsh was referring to Will's position that integrationists and segregationists were equally entitled to the grace of God.

In November 1985 Orlando Bagwell of Blackside, Inc. interviewed Will about how the white and black churches in Montgomery reacted to the worst part of the Freedom Rider crisis. Just one day after the students arrived in the city, Will was attempting to visit hospitals where the students, some in critical condition, were located. He kept turning the radio knob and listening to one church broadcast after the other. He could have been on a different planet as far as hearing news of the violence the day before. In the white church, the sermons sought no forgiveness nor deliverance. The black churches were holding services every night; but if black preachers had been on the radio during the daytime, they would have mentioned the violence in prayer, praise, homily, and psalm. The institutional churches were concerned about the appearance of harmony in their congregations.

Ben Hartley, author of "Radical Christian" in a June 21, 1971, issue of *Presbyterian Survey* magazine, questioned Will about the makeup of his flock. People criticized Will because he counseled with Klan members. Will pointed out that the lowest and least were also the children of God. Will did not work with the Klan, but if they were sick or in jail he visited them. He met with leaders from both sides during the riots in an effort to avoid violence. He also visited with black people, people in the music business, and counseled with people in the drug culture. Human beings of all races and economic and cultural levels felt that Will was accessible.

Walter B. Clancy, in his article "Jesus in the Brush Arbor: An Interview with Will Campbell" (*New Orleans Review*), asked Will about "the southern tragedy" which Will described as two groups, black and white, living side by side. Each came from a different kind of bondage; the blacks from the worst kind of slavery and the whites as indentured servants from Europe. Had they united, they could have forged a strong political and economic force. However, they continued to be enemies. The indentured servants could have been free after seven or so years, but free to what and to where? The planter classes played the poor whites against the blacks and kept the whites in their places by fear of intermarriage.

Even during the heat of the civil rights movement, Will continued to write books and perform weddings, funerals, baptisms, home visits, and jail visits without pay. Throughout his life, he never agreed to TV evangelism or syndicated speaking tours. That was not his understanding with Mr. Jesus, as Will sometimes called Jesus, about Christian preaching.

After Rev. King's 1963 letter from a Birmingham jail focused on what he believed was blindness to the movement by moderates and the church, the old Council of Southern Churchmen met in 1964 and changed the organization's name to Committee of Southern Churchmen. The organization became a committee because Will preferred it that way. Campbell was the leading person or preacher at large. The purpose of the organization was to renew the spread of 2 Corinthians 5:11–21—if He loves one, He loves all.

This radical concept had changed Will's ministry. After a part-time deputy sheriff killed a young activist ministerial student, Will faced his own professed belief. He had popularized, in a conversation with a friend, the statement "We are all equal in the eyes of God" to "We are all bastards but God loves us anyway." Will believed that Caesar's law, a jury, had erroneously exonerated the shooter. The unarmed victim, a young ministerial student who was in the county trying to register voters, was walking out of a country store when the shotgun blast ended his life. Was the shooter a "bastard"? Yes. Was the victim a "bastard"? It wrenched Will's soul to say "yes." However, he knew he could not, as a preacher, second-guess the scriptures as to the worth of any human being, nor limit his care to those he personally deemed worthy. As bitter as it was to swallow when he was still grieving the young man's death, he had to recognize that all human beings are flawed, but all are equal recipients of grace and reconciliation.

In an interview for *Oxford American* in 1997, Frye Gaillard and Will talked about Will's book *And Also with You: Duncan Gray and the American Dilemma*. This biography defines the "American Dilemma" as racism. The book further amplifies Will's theology as to grace and reconciliation. Many students of Campbell recognized connections between some of Will's prose and his core religious beliefs. Duncan Gray was the Mississippi Episcopal priest (later a bishop) who went to the Ole Miss campus in 1964 and pled for calm during the riots when federal marshals were called to register the first black man, James Meredith, to the University of Mississippi. Ironically, Gray spoke from upon a civil war statue. Will praised Duncan Gray for stating that a religion of true faith in Jesus must lead a preacher to the people as opposed to TV evangelism. Will called the Duncan Gray book a sermon. Many readers would urge that Campbell's books *Cecilia's Sin*, *Glad River*, and *Brother to a Dragonfly* are like teaching or preaching. Will was more a teacher than an old-time preacher. He never threatened anyone with hell or tried to persuade or save them with overbearing rhetoric.

The Committee of Southern Churchmen (CSC) was the last institution for which Will worked. The *Katallagete* (Greek for "being reconciled") was Will's high-powered journal of the CSC and was highly effective. Will Campbell was its heart and soul, according to Jennifer Ford ("Will Campbell and Christ's Ambassadors: Selections from the *Katallagete/* James Y. Holloway Special Collections, University of Mississippi," *Journal of Southern Religion*).

From the time Will ended his employment with the CSC in 1963, he worked at writing and preaching from his log cabin at Mount Juliet, Tennessee. He also lectured across the country and was much in demand. Many scholars, including a close friend of Will's, John Egerton, described Campbell as personal preacher to an eclectic group of unconventional Christians who were ignored and left out by the institutional church.

Located near Liberty, Mississippi, Will's childhood church, East Fork Baptist Church, through baptism and ordination, gave Will the permanent authority to be a preacher without needing the institutional church. Will based his ministry on Second Corinthians and Galatians 3. To Will, Jesus was a real presence, as gentle as a lamb and as palpable as a lightning strike on the East Fork River. Awesome duties and responsibilities flowed from Will's application of the radical teaching of Jesus Christ.

Will was also likeable and funny. He did say the rich churches in America should be torn down and sold to raise money to feed, clothe, house, and provide medicine for the poor. However, we must remember that Will was an English major at Wake Forest. He, a spellbinding speaker, knew rhetorical tools, including irony, satire, humor, timing, sarcasm, understatement, and overstatement. He had of course read Jonathan Swift's *A Modest Proposal*, published in 1729. As a preacher, he never forgot audience impact; and as a prophet, he spoke in plain emotive words. However, he did not hope to clank a Caterpillar bulldozer toward First Baptist of Gotham City. Nor did Swift want to use homo sapiens as food for the poor. But each hoped to focus attention toward serious concerns.

He was often witty and sometimes subtle. He would introduce his wife, Brenda, by saying (for example), "Hello, Mr. Jones. This is my first wife, Brenda." He would not laugh or wink. Jones would have to catch on or not. A favorite was, "Nice to see you, Mr. Jones; see you again a while ago."

He wrote many successful books but no bestsellers. Therefore, he would tell an audience at a speech that he was Will D. Campbell, author of rare books. After a pause, Will would add dismissively that rare books just came to him naturally. He did not even have to work at it. Some would figure it out. Others would continue to admire the first rare book writer they ever saw. When people accused him of being anti-intellectual, he would say he was not intellectual enough to be anti-intellectual.

The *Wittenburg Door* sent Bill McNabb, its most experienced interviewer, to see Will in 1990. They enjoyed testing each other. After reminding Will that "we do have steeples and institutions," and "almost all of us belong to them," McNabb asked Will whether he was for tearing them all down. Will said it would not do any good if he did. Someone would build them right back. Christianity and religion were not synonymous. However, he was not against religion nor Christianity nor churches. Churches are not buildings. Christian worship is the church. If "the Church" as built by Mr. Jesus were finite, somebody would locate and commercialize it.

Will found nothing in the Old or New Testament that dealt with setting up a society or a civilization, nor could he set up one. He could not be a "Christian congressman." Will denies being anarchistic and points out that anarchy is political and not Christian. Emphasizing that he did not want to set up any society, Will maintained that he could do no better than Nixon, Ford, or Roosevelt. He only wanted to talk in terms of Christian responses, wherever it might be, according to Orley B. Caudill.

From 1962 through 2012, Brother Campbell published thirteen books including novels, biographies, and an autobiography. *Brother to a Dragonfly*, his autobiography, was a National Book Award finalist and winner of the Lillian Smith Prize and the Christopher Award. *The Glad River* won a first-place award from the Friends of American Writers in 1982. His works have also won a Lyndhurst Prize and an Alex Haley Award.

In 2000 Mike Letcher produced *God's Will*, a TV documentary for University of Alabama Center for Public TV and Radio. Those well-produced episodes about his life were narrated by Ossie Davis and are available online at https://vimeo.com/55126898. Mike Letcher was kind enough to allow our use of Interview #21. There Will discussed his writing more freely than ever before, to my knowledge. Will, who was a preacher without a pulpit, confided that his writing was indeed his pulpit. Though it was unintentional, everything he wrote was about the search for community or reconciliation, which as we know is the heart of Will's ministry. Will said, "There is no such thing as 'complete fiction.'" Though he is not "up to anything," he knows that "the writing comes out of who I am. It all comes from some experience."

His brother Joe, a pharmacist, chose methamphetamines to feel better. The Confederacy chose racism to feel superior to black people. Each course of behavior gave a false sense of well-being. Each choice was wrong and tragic, causing death to Joe and to the Confederacy. Will was a victim of those two different but compulsive choices. The South was a victim of the choice of the Confederacy. Though *Brother To a Dragon Fly* was about Will's struggle with those two destructive choices, he did not realize it until scores of years later.

Will did not call himself a writer because he felt as if it would have been presumptuous since he could not write full time. Emergencies in his ministry caused too many interruptions. He considered writing almost a hobby. His ministry to people was the first thing.

The Glad River is his better-written book, but *Brother to a Dragonfly* is so nearly sacred. It was "painful and rewarding." Will's tragic brother Joe's first wife sued Will unsuccessfully for three quarters of a million dollars for slander and libel against her in *Brother to a Dragonfly*. Will said that experience was "depressing almost in the clinical sense." He could not deal with it and he could not figure out why she did it. However, he knew if there was anything libelous, slanderous, or vicious in that book, all writers might as well melt their typewriters, as Will stated in *God's Will*.

In 2003, *The Glad River* was rereleased by Smith and Helwys to great acclaim. Reviewers called Will Campbell's religious books readable from a Christian worldview, citing *The Glad River, Brother to a Dragonfly, Soul among Lions, Musings of a Bootleg Preacher, Forty Acres and a Goat,* and *Providence.* Interviewer Bob Flynn wrote, "Will Campbell was said to be a traditional Baptist who knew that scriptural perversion was worse than sexual diversion, and that greed was worse than bourbon. He was a gentle iconoclast . . . who happily smashed his idols."

Campbell insisted that his ministry was a calling, not an occupation. We understand Campbell better by recognizing how much he was influenced by Liberty, Mississippi's East Fork Baptist Church, his ordination there, Joe, his family tragedies, and the reality of that environment and its teachings. He did not care that neither institutional churches nor denominations recognized the authenticity of his ordination. He placed the certificate, a plain piece of paper, typed and signed by the young preacher who ordained him, and by Will's daddy, his cousin, and his uncle, on his wall. Never mind the misspelled words and typos. He deliberately covered the faces of the documents from Tulane and Yale by taping the church ordination certificate over them, according to Ken Gibble in his interview "Living Out the Drama" (*Presbyterian Survey Magazine*, June 21, 1971).

During the sixties, Will was invited to speak at a ceremony in the East Fork Church. Opposition church members were trying to withdraw or invalidate the ordination certificate. They threatened to kill him if he came to the church. Will's father and brother Joe warned Will to stay away, but he was resolved to go. Will's friends intervened on his behalf and got the death threat lifted. The rescue group's most interesting note stated that if Will came to harm, his friends would "filibuster the church to the ground." Apparently the note worked.

After becoming friends with Walker Percy and Flannery O'Connor, Will saw the peacocks that Ms. O'Connor kept on her farm. Will was fond of his own chickens called guinea hens. He told Kenneth Gibble with the *Christian Century*, while discussing writing, that the only difference between himself and O'Connor was that she raised peacocks and he raised guinea hens. Apparently, on a roll during the interview, while discussing education in America, he boasted about insisting that all three of his children have a degree from at least one institution of higher learning. This was because he wanted them to know the difference between the humor of Polonius and that of Minnie Pearl, and the difference between Beaujolais and Ripple wine.

Walker Percy told Will the only way to write a novel was to "sacrifice your senses to the brink of total insanity" and then finish it, then see what can be salvaged of your senses. His point was that Will was too busy in his ministering to people to do that. Will is fond of saying that Percy pestered him about mixing a Christian baptism with a romantic baptism in a draft of *The Glad River*. Will said Percy used a lot of unclear Latin about the heresy and the efficacy of the baptism not depending on the goodness of the priest. Percy said that mistake would hurt the novel. So Will had the character Kingston tell the character Doops, who was refusing baptism, to go ahead because it didn't matter whether the priest was an SOB or not. Percy called Will late one night after he had seen the change in the published book and told Will it was "one hell of a novel." "Now you know how scholarly criticism works," Will said.

Will was thirty years old and still a preacher without a church and without financial security when he moved to Nashville in 1955. He refused suggestions to form his own church or to become a TV preacher. Entrepreneurs offered to syndicate him as a lecturer, but he remained a preacher who did what he could for his flock without pay because that was his agreement with Mr. Jesus.

Ken Carder, a retired Methodist bishop in both Tennessee and Mississippi, and a man of countless steeples, published an article June 18, 2013, following Campbell's death. Carder eulogized Campbell, stating that "the man who was suspicious of creeds lived by that radical creed [the teachings of Jesus] . . . who mistrusted institutions, challenged them to incorporate . . . God's righteousness and justice . . . he made institutions better, helping to transform them and the world in which we lived . . . helped me to know myself as a child of God."

Dr. Merrill Hawkins Jr. wrote his PhD dissertation based on discussions with Campbell about his works. He observed that Will's fictional writings are both religious and autobiographical. Campbell understood the cultural and the religious as a southerner. "His words continue to make a positive contribution to the human experience," stated Dr. Hawkins, whose book, *Will Campbell: Radical Prophet of the South*, was published by Mercer University Press in 1997.

"Will Campbell, preacher, writer, lecturer, raconteur, social iconoclast, and equal-opportunity prophet, died in Nashville on Monday, June 3, 2013," wrote Bill Leonard in an article, "The Freedom of Will," in the *Associated Baptist Press*, June 4, 2013.

• • •

I thank those authors and publishers who allowed us to publish their works in this volume. I thank Will's family and his good friend Tom T. Hall for helping Judge Robert Evans and me schedule Will for a final interview. We all had lunch together at a favorite roadhouse in Mount Juliet before beginning. Will asked why we needed another interview. Tom T. told him it would be a visit with friends where he could tell stories folks would like to share. Will, after a pause, said he reckoned he and Bob and I could "tell lies" for a couple of days.

I thank Rita Royals for her tireless efforts in requesting permissions and in background research. I also thank my friend Ed Becker for giving us time from his computer software business. His English literature education at Vanderbilt University was an asset in reading and editing. I want to thank Webb Campbell, Will's son, a top-flight litigation attorney with the Sherrod and Roe Law Firm in Nashville, Tennessee, for taking the time to talk to me. I thank Courtney Warner, a senior public management major at Millsaps College for her assistance with proofing and the computer. She succeeded

Ryan Hamilton, an English major and computer wizard who recently graduated from Millsaps College.

I thank the University Press of Mississippi for letting me edit this book. I especially thank my editor, Katie Keene, for her astute guidance. Seetha Srinivasan and Valerie Jones provided valuable assistance. The Mississippi Library Commission librarians were most helpful in ordering from libraries across the nation. Staff members of the University of Southern Mississippi libraries assisted us in researching the many folders of Will Campbell's donated papers. Millsaps College librarians were extremely helpful in research, also. Rosie McNair was a staunch supporter for the entire venture.

Rita and I were honored to have Will Campbell as a friend for many years. This work makes us miss you, Brother Will. We will see you a while ago.

TR

References

Bagwell, Orlando. "Interview with Reverend Will Campbell." In *Eyes on the Prize: America's Civil Rights Years, 1954–1965*. Blackside, Inc., Washington University Libraries, Film and Media Archive, November 3, 1985.

Carder, Kenneth. "Bubba to a Gadfly—Remembering Will D. Campbell." *Faith and Leadership*, June 18, 2013. https://www.faithandleadership.com/content/ken-carder-bubba-gadfly-remembering-will-d-campbell.

Caudill, Orley B. *An Oral History with Will Davis Campbell, Christian Preacher*. The Mississippi Oral History Program, vol. 157. Hattiesburg: University of Southern Mississippi, 1980, 33–53, 86–100.

Clancy, Walter B. "Jesus in the Brush Arbor: An Interview with Will Campbell." *New Orleans Review* 4, no. 3 (1974): 228–31.

Egerton, John. "Reverend Will D. Campbell, Southern Racial Reconciler." *Southern Spaces*, June 2013.

Fast, Howard. *Freedom Road*. New York: Routledge, 1944. Reprinted with an introduction by Eric Foner and foreword by W. E. B. Du Bois. New York: Routledge, 1995.

Flynn, Bob. "Interview with Will D. Campbell." *Wittenburg Door*, November/December 2003.

Ford, Jennifer. "Will Campbell and Christ's Ambassadors: Selections from the *Katallagete/* James Y. Holloway Collection, Special Collections, University of Mississippi." *Journal of Southern Religion*, August 2000. http://jsr.fsu.edu/ford.htm.

Gaillard, Frye. "Will Campbell." *Oxford American*, issue 19 (Winter 1997): 76–77.

Gaillard, Frye. "Appreciating Will Campbell, 'Preacher to the Damned.'" *The Progressive*, April 2014.

Gibble, Ken. "Living Out the Drama: An Interview with Will Campbell." *Christian Century*, May 30, 1984.

Hartley, Ben. "Radical Christian: An Interview with Will D. Campbell." *Presbyterian Survey Magazine*, June 21, 1971.

Hawkins, Merrill M. *Will Campbell: Radical Prophet of the South*. Macon, Ga.: Mercer University Press, 1977.

Houston, Benjamin. "An Interview with Will D. Campbell." *Journal of Southern Religion*, July 1, 2003.

Letcher, Mike. *God's Will*. University of Alabama Center for Public TV & Radio, 2000. https://vimeo.com/55126898.

Marsh, Charles. "Interview by Charles Marsh." Transcription of audio recording, July 6, 1993. Doc #7INT24. Project on Lived Theology Civil Rights Paper Archive.

McNabb, Bill. "The Futility of Fighting Over What We Believe." *Wittenburg Door*, no. 110 (March/April 1990).

Prather, Paul. "Preacher Contrasts Religion, Christianity." *Lexington Herald Leader*, November 12, 1992.

Royals, Tom, and Bob Evans. "Interview with Will Davis Campbell." December 9, 2009. Previously unpublished.

Chronology

1924	Will D. Campbell is born on July 18, in Liberty, Amite County, Mississippi, to Lee Webb and Hancie Bea (Parker) Campbell.
1941	Graduates from high school and is ordained as a Baptist minister in the East Fork Baptist church.
1941	Attends Louisiana College in Pineville, Louisiana, until 1943.
1943–46	Serves in the Pacific Theater in the United States Army as a combat medic and reaches rank of sergeant.
1946	Marries Brenda Fisher on January 16, and moves to North Carolina. The couple goes on to have one son, Webb, and two daughters, Penny and Bonnie.
1948	Receives bachelor of arts degree in English from Wake Forest College.
1948	Moves to New Orleans and attends Tulane University for graduate study until 1949.
1952	Receives a bachelor of divinity degree from Yale Divinity School.
1952–54	Serves as pastor at Taylor Southern Baptist Church in Taylor, Louisiana.
1954–56	Works as director of religious life and chaplain at the University of Mississippi. Campbell resigns after receiving death threats due to integrationist views.
1956–63	Moves to Nashville and works as field director for the National Council of Churches.
1957	Campbell is among only four white ministers escorting African American students desegregating Little Rock Central High School. Campbell is the only white person invited by Dr. Martin Luther King Jr. and who attended the founding of the Southern Christian Leadership Conference (SCLC) at Ebenezer Baptist Church in Atlanta.
1961	Joins Congress of Racial Equality (CORE) and the Student Nonviolent Coordinating Committee (SNCC) Freedom Riders to integrate bus travel.

1962   Publishes his first book, *Race and the Renewal of the Church.*

1963–72 Works as preacher at large for the Committee of Southern Churchmen and editor and publisher of *The Katallagete.*

1963   Joins Dr. Martin Luther King Jr. in Birmingham sit-ins, marches, and boycotts.

1965   Joins Dr. Martin Luther King Jr. in the Selma to Montgomery marches.

1968   Campbell is present at the Lorraine Motel on April 4, the night Dr. Martin Luther King Jr. is assassinated. Later, Campbell meets King's murderer, James Earl Ray, in prison.

1977   Publishes *Brother to a Dragonfly.* It is named one of the best books of the year by the *New York Times,* wins the Lillian Smith Prize and the Christopher Award, and becomes a finalist for the National Book Award.

1981   *Kudzu,* a daily comic strip by Doug Marlette, debuts featuring a character modeled after Campbell—Rev. Will B. Dunn. The comic is syndicated in three hundred newspapers and runs through 2007.

1982   Publishes *The Glad River.* It wins a first-place award from the Friends of American Writers.

1983   Publishes *Cecelia's Sin.*

1984   Campbell receives an honorary degree from Wake Forest University.

1986   Publishes *Forty Acres and a Goat.*

1989   Publishes *Covenant: Faces, Voices, Places* and *Chester and Chun Ling.*

1991   Publishes *The Convention: A Parable.*

1992   Publishes *Providence.* Campbell is awarded the Alex Haley Memorial Award for distinguished Tennessee writers.

1993   Receives an honorary degree from the University of the South.

1994   Campbell is awarded the Tennessee Governor's Award for the Arts.

1995   Publishes *The Stem of Jesse: The Costs of Community at a 1960s Southern School.* Campbell is awarded the Tennessee Governor's Humanities Award.

1996   Publishes *The Pear Tree that Bloomed in the Fall.* Campbell receives an honorary degree from Mercer University.

1997   Publishes *And Also with You: Duncan Gray and the American Dilemma; Bluebirds Always Come on Sunday;* and *Shugah and*

Doops. Is awarded a Lifetime Achievement Award from the American Civil Liberties Union (Tennessee chapter).

1998   Is awarded the Richard Wright Prize at the Natchez Literary Celebration and first prize in nonfiction from the Mississippi Institute of Arts and Letters.

1999   Publishes *Soul among Lions: Musings of a Bootleg Preacher.* Campbell receives an honorary degree from the University of Southern Mississippi.

2000   Is awarded a National Humanities Medal by President William J. Clinton. The Public Broadcasting Service (PBS) broadcasts *God's Will*, a documentary based on Campbell's life narrated by Ossie Davis.

2003   Publishes *Robert G. Clark's Journey to the House: A Black Politician's Story.*

2007   Is awarded the William Sloane Coffin Award for Peace and Justice from Yale Divinity School.

2011   Suffers a disabling stroke.

2012   Wake Forest inducts Campbell into the Wake Forest Writers Hall of Fame.

2013   At eighty-eight years old, Campbell passes away from complications following a stroke.

Conversations with Will D. Campbell

Radical Christian: An Interview with Rev. Will Campbell

Ben Hartley / 1971

This article was originally published in the June 21, 1971, issue of *Presbyterian Survey*, a former publication of the Presbyterian Church (USA), and is reprinted here with permission.

Ben Hartley: When did you first discern that you didn't exactly fit into the lifestyle of Mississippians?

Will Campbell: I never was uncomfortable there—you see, I didn't exactly leave by choice. I was ready to spend the rest of my life there. I would have been content to stay there.

Ben Hartley: How did you get involved with the Committee of Southern Churchmen?

Will Campbell: Well, I was at Ole Miss as chaplain and got in a little trouble there, and went to work for the National Council of Churches and got in a little trouble with them; some friends wanted to re-tread the old Fellowship of Southern Churchmen. And I wanted to stay in the South.

Ben Hartley: Who do you minister to?

Will Campbell: I don't like to use the term, ministry—the term is a pretty presumptuous one. I have a relationship, a human relationship with a number of different types and some of these have been romanticized and over-dramatized, like this bit about working with the Ku Klux Klan. I don't work with them, but I know some people who are active in the Klan and when their folks get sick I go over there and help take care of them. I just do whatever I can for 'em. Or when they go to jail I go over there and play my guitar and we have a little communion service. Heretical, perhaps, but there's nothing really far out about it, nothing pious about it.

Ben Hartley: Other relationships?

Will Campbell: I have that kind of thing with some black people, as well. And I know some people in the music business. And I've gotten into this drug culture thing.

Ben Hartley: And that's what the Committee of Southern Churchmen is about?

Will Campbell: Well, if you had to define the areas of activity of the committee, it is a ministry of aid to minority groups. Folks that are lost or estranged. This means the program is pretty broad, spread pretty thin. But it was Jesus who spread it thin. You see, he didn't say *which* prisoners to visit—black or white—guilt or not guilty—*which* sick, *which* poor to bring good news to, deserving or underserving.

Ben Hartley: You have a new program going?

Will Campbell: Yes, we call it a program for victims of militarism—to those who have deserted to Canada and other places, but especially to their families. When I went to Canada the first time, I talked rather naively to some of those fellows about "getting amnesty" for them. And they told me they were interested in amnesty too, but for the folks in the US because they didn't feel like they had done anything but that the government and the people who support it had committed the crimes. So we feel that the real brokenness is on this side of the border.

Ben Hartley: This includes families of boys who have been killed?

Will Campbell: Yes. There's great frustration and grief—not just because they have lost their sons—but because they feel down deep that their boy may have died for no good reason. It wasn't like this in World War II when people put a gold star flag in their window with considerable pride, even though they might be grief-stricken. They could live with this. But the Vietnam thing is different. You talk about alienation and brokenness—here it is!

Ben Hartley: And families of draft evaders?

Will Campbell: Like the letter from the mother of a boy waiting up on the Canadian border for the results of his final appeal to his draft board. Deep down she agreed with what he was doing but it was an embarrassing situation in the community. This is the kind of thing that is tearing the country apart.

Ben Hartley: Are you a pacifist?

Will Campbell: I'm not a pacifist and I'm not a non-pacifist. As a sinner I know I could be goaded into violence, but I don't parade my sin as a virtue. Love of country is not the same as love for God.

Ben Hartley: You made some headlines recently when you blasted Billy Graham. Why did you want to do that?

Will Campbell: We didn't blast Billy Graham. We called him a "court prophet" and we stand by that. But the thing not understood about our letter to Dr. Graham is that the liberal often tips that hat to this or that Caesar, not a Nixon or a Wallace, but perhaps a Humphrey or a Johnson and is thus just as much a court prophet. Caesar is Caesar no matter the label or name.

Ben Hartley: So do you believe in evangelism?

Will Campbell: Brother, it's all evangelism!

Ben Hartley: That's not a Baptist's answer, is it?

Will Campbell: Depends on what kind of Baptist you're talking about. Evangelism isn't asking people to join something. It's inviting them to *be* something. Evangelism is not building a kingdom, it's abiding in one already built.

Ben Hartley: A lot of people look at you as a liberal because you're an activist. But somehow you manage to maintain dialogue with all kinds of people. What are you?

Will Campbell: I get sort of impatient with people who sit around analyzing and asking themselves. "Who am I?" I know who I am. Certainly what I am saying doesn't infer any kind of feeling of perfection or satisfaction with myself as a great guy. I'm happy in my frailty because Jesus loves me. Hallelujah! I know I'm just one more slob, but I don't worry about it and analyze what makes me like this or that. I can't be very tolerant of piety because of the legalism—the don'ts. But the legalism of the liberal can be even more vicious and even more pietistic. And thus is still a works righteousness.

Ben Hartley: But the Gospel is something different from what you do or don't do. What is the Gospel?

Will Campbell: The Gospel is the Good News that God was in Christ no longer holding men's misdeeds against them. Now that is tough. That means you're going to have to go down there in Alabama and tell Thomas Coleman, the guy who killed Jonathan Daniels because he was registering black people to vote, that God sets him free just like the State of Alabama did. Jesus said this. He said you're free—go sin no more—you don't have to do this.

Ben Hartley: People representing different positions in the denominations—conservatives and liberals—seem to be locked into win-lose battles from which they cannot be extricated and reconciled. How do you feel about this polarization? Where will it lead us?

Will Campbell: Nowhere. I really don't think it makes any difference. I have—and I'm happy with this—despaired of institutional Christianity; I have despaired of the steeples. You can merge together in COCU, and it doesn't make any difference. I think it would be kind of nice because it's silly having all these spearing things called denominations. You could merge all the morgues in town, and you don't get a single living body. And it seems to me that the institutional church often bears not Good News but bad. When the crucifixion didn't work, we tried to institutionalize Jesus, but that won't work either for he is rising up all over the place. And in some places far removed from the steeple.

Ben Hartley: But let me draw one of these issues more realistically. One group says, "You haven't got faith unless you manifest your love for your brother in these ways—you've got to do as well as believe, if you claim to be a Christian." And the conservative seems to say, "Don't think you're going to make it with God, because you want a better deal for the black man in this country. What we've got to do is get people committed to Jesus Christ, the crucified and risen Lord." This is the way the battle lines are drawn.

Will Campbell: I would have to come down on the side of the conversation IF they want to talk about what this means: that Jesus no longer holds man's misdeeds against him and it means when we are in Christ, we no longer judge men in human terms—color, national boundaries, etc.—where these human categories don't count anymore. If that's what the conservatives mean, I'm right in their camp, brother! I'm with them and they think they're absolutely right when they say to the liberal that he ain't going to cut it because he goes around mouthing about loving black people. The liberals have done it to the black people more than the conservatives because the liberals have had the power.

Ben Hartley: And would that be true of the war, too?

Will Campbell: Yes, sir, this is the liberals' war. Barry Goldwater said what he would do, and we went around saying that we had to stop the anti-Christ. But then by golly, we got the anti-Christ who did far more than Barry Goldwater was even thinking about.

Ben Hartley: But are the liberals saying that you got it made with Jesus if you treat your black brothers right? And I don't hear the conservatives saying that if you just love Jesus everything's going to be all right. But this is what they're accusing one another of saying. And the people in the middle are wishy-washy and don't want to deal with the issues that the two sides are raising. So where does this leave us?

Will Campbell: I don't consider myself in the middle. But the issue *is* Christ crucified and risen. This means we don't any longer measure men by human standards. God didn't create the USA and South Vietnam—we did, man did. He created the St. Lawrence and the Rio Grande River and the Pacific Ocean and then we came along and used 'em to say, "That part's ours and that's yours." National boundaries are human categories. Race is another. Now if they want to consider some radical international relations or radical race relations—liberals or conservatives—they will have only to read II Corinthians 5 and they will find it. But goodbye white America if we take that bit seriously!

Ben Hartley: Let's talk about some radical evangelism.

Will Campbell: That's what I've been talking about. I'm talking about God in Christ who put an end to human categories. That's dangerous stuff— more than I'm ready to buy.

Ben Hartley: But we're all hung up with these things?

Will Campbell: That's right. Liberals and conservatives alike.

Ben Hartley: But your ministry to deserters in Canada—that makes you a liberal. The conservatives aren't going to accept those other words you use because you've proved you didn't mean them by aiding deserters.

Will Campbell: Like I said, deserting a man-made national boundary isn't the same as deserting God—we have confused the two too long. And even if they had deserted God, he loves them all the more—remember the Prodigal story.

Ben Hartley: And you have a ministry to the KKK?

Will Campbell: More like they have a ministry to me. I once asked a Klan leader what they stood for. He said, "For peace, harmony, and freedom." We talked at length about what he meant when he used these words. And we agreed that in reality *he* defined the words. Then I asked him what means he was willing to use to achieve those glorious ends. He said: "Burning, bombing, killing, torture—whatever it takes." I thought I had him until he asked me what we stand for in Vietnam, who defines the words we use, and what methods we use to achieve the goals. That Klansman was my prophet, brother. The ministry was to me.

Ben Hartley: Who was the Klan chief you went to prison with?

Will Campbell: Bob Jones.

Ben Hartley: Did he run a school of some kind?

Will Campbell: No, this is J. R. Jones. He went to prison for contempt of Congress for not letting them see the Klan's records.

Ben Hartley: Why do you whittle all the time? And chew gum?

Will Campbell: I started chewing gum when I quit chewing tobacco a couple of months ago.

Ben Hartley: And what about the whittling?

Will Campbell: Maybe Nero was right. Maybe the time for whittling has come.

Jesus in the Brush Arbor:
An Interview with Will Campbell

Walter B. Clancy / 1974

From *New Orleans Review* 4, no. 3 (1974): 228–31. Reprinted with permission of Mark Yakich, editor, *New Orleans Review*.

A noted theologian, graduate of Yale University, and commentator on the South, Mr. Campbell is the author of numerous articles and books which reflect his concern with the southern religious experience. This interview was recently conducted by Walter B. Clancy, on special assignment for the *New Orleans Review*, at Mr. Campbell's home near Nashville, Tennessee. Dr. Clancy is former president of the Southern Churchmen and presently professor of social welfare at the University of Arkansas's Graduate School of Social Work in Little Rock.

Walter B. Clancy: First of all, can we speak of a "Southern Experience"? Is there an identifiable subculture of the South?

Will Campbell: Yes, I think there is such a thing as the "Southern Experience" and we can speak of it. At least we can speak in the spirit of it—I am not sure we can verbalize what it is. I know it is more than just the fact that the South lost a war. I know it did not arise because the South owned slaves. America and the South pretty much brought that practice and that era to a close in the community of nations, but it was not unique with us and certainly we did not originate it. I know that it was not and is not simply the agrarian influence. Other parts of the nation were and are more rural than the South, and Rogation Sunday was not put on the Church calendars by the Georgia Grange. In short, every single historical factor which may be used to sum up the South or explain the southern experience can be duplicated in other regions or in other nations. And yet no other region in this nation, and I suspect any nation, is quite so distinct, so identifiable, with a history as a separate academic discipline from American history or history in general, with schools of literature, and politics, mores, and behavior patterns. Now, of course, all that is changing, has already changed, and it is questionable in most circles to speak of "The South" anymore. But there was a southern experience and vestiges remain and there are holdouts who are not willing to give it up to the world of Howard Johnsons and McDonald hamburgers. And it is interesting to me that it is not the bigots who are the holdouts for the most part, but the romantics and those loosely called progressives who never equated "The Southern Way of Life" with racial discrimination. Those who did and still do equate "The Southern Way of Life" with racial discrimination seem seldom to oppose the coming of the roads, strip mining, technology, urbanization, the disappearance of the small farm, and all the rest. Leander Perez might scream "nigger! nigger!" to the point of near excommunication, but I do not recall his resisting the encroachment—federal or otherwise—of industrialization in his Louisiana parishes. But just what the "Southern Experience" is I would be afraid to try to sum up. What produced the Faulkners, Weltys, O'Connors, Percys, etc.? Is it just the fact that we were a defeated and suffering people? I think not. If so, where are the literary figures of the vast majority of the world which is also defeated and suffering? Harry Williams suggests that the two most radical political figures in American history, Huey Long and Lyndon Johnson, were southerners, and he implies that they could only have been southerners, despite the fact that the South is generally considered the most conservative area of the nation. Why? And certainly it takes more than injustice to explain the rise of the civil rights movement, for the demon of injustice is as alive on the Lower East Side of New York City as it is in Alabama or Mississippi. Maybe the term "Southern Experience" should read "Southern Tragedy."

Clancy: What do you see as the southern tragedy? Was it the war and its aftermath of economics and politics or is it something else?
Campbell: The southern tragedy, in my judgment, is that here we had two groups of people, one black, one white, living side-by-side, both in the same boat, both having come here as servants or slaves, who if they had ever banded together could have taken over the country. But instead they have continued to this very day to be the enemy of each other.

Clancy: You will have to take me a little further. I don't understand the bit about each group being slaves. Was that not an experience which only the blacks had?

Campbell: Well, certainly they had the experience to a larger degree. But I believe that one of the historical factors in the bleak racial picture in America which has never been dealt with fully is the matter of indentured servanthood so common during the early days of this country. "Serve me for five years or seven years and I will give you passage to the new country and then I will set you free." But freedom to what and in what context? Freedom to flounder, to wander westward and try to scratch out a living in a wilderness and in competition with the gentry with large holdings, good education, and free slave labor. Certainly not all the poor whites, wool hats, peckerwoods, rednecks, etc., are offsprings of indentured servants. But a lot of us are. And if the origins of our history were to be played down as we taught our children, then the slave origins of others, in this case, the blacks, had to be played up. Plus the fact that the two groups were played off against each other. Tell the rednecks that if they persist in their egalitarian activities in such things as the Populist movement, the Farmer's Alliance, or even the Long regimes of the thirties, forties, and fifties, their daughters will be ravished by black bucks. And thus far he has always backed away.

Clancy: What does Religion as opposed to the Church have to contribute positively to the southern experience?

Campbell: Well, Walter, I guess it will be necessary for us at this point to define some terms or we're going to misunderstand each other. You are a cradle Catholic talking to a deep-water Baptist. I think I know what you mean by "Religion" and "Church" and I have no quarrel with your usage. But I am not sure that my thought patterns are the same. I gather that when you use the term "Religion" you use it in a positive way. And when you use the term "Church" perhaps you are not thinking so positively. Or maybe it is the other way around. Anyway, I do not use either of these terms in a favorable light. I might use the term "Gospel" where you are using "Religion." I believe that our Lord was among the most antireligious ever to come along, for He came breaking the rules, smashing idols, tearing down structures, and proclaiming freedom from all such. And rules, crusades, and structures are the stuff religion is made of, whereas Jesus came proclaiming deliverance. I grew up in the Protestant tradition which was alleged in the beginning to espouse that deliverance from the prison house of structures. But, of course, it didn't work out that way. No religious group in the world is now more structure-bound than American Protestant groups. And when I use the term "Church," I am thinking of those institutions which make and enforce the religious rules. (Now when I use the term "The Church" I am thinking of what Jesus said that He would establish and did establish. But it does not depend for its existence or efficacy upon buildings, promotional schemes, names, places, computers, etc., etc. It is simply a relationship, the believers acting out the "Good News," the Gospel of deliverance from sin and death.) So, I suppose my answer would have to be that both Religion and Church have contributed negatively to the southern experience. It was, after all, Religion and Church which provided the moral and ethical justification for slavery. And it was also, after all, Religion and Church which provided the morale which sustained the Civil War, long after the southern cause would have collapsed otherwise. Certainly that is not the same as saying that "Gospel" did those things. And we can look back now and say that there was nothing Christian in those things. I have appreciated and learned so much from Walker Percy on this point: his insistence that southern religion during that era was Stoic and not Christian says a lot.

Clancy: Some say the churches were the principal instrumentalities in molding the "Mind of the South." Do you agree?

Campbell: Yes. And then, no. Religion as discussed by Percy certainly did do much in that direction. But that was the religion of the aristocracy, of the very few. But the religion discussed by Cash and others, I believe, had no such influence. In fact it didn't even exist. Nothing, I think, has been so grossly exaggerated as the religiosity of the rural South prior to the Civil War. It was not religious. The aristocracy had their chaplains from Canterbury and Geneva, and yes, sometimes from Rome, though not as often, but the masses had the occasional visits from the circuit rider preachers on their way from Philadelphia to Natchez, the half-remembered biblical quotes from those visits, old wives' tales, all mixed with Indian lore and some carryover from the religious tradition of their ancestors—which wasn't much because those brought over as indentured servants were not apt to be those steeped in Christian theology or any other kind of theology. Now these people were recruited and enlisted for war and given religious instruction simultaneously. And when the war was over and they were once more on their own, they would do much with their religious teachings. But by then the "Mind of the South" was pretty much made up. The religious conversion by the chaplains of the Confederacy included the rightness of slavery and the inherent inferiority of the blacks. And this carried over. But it was not Redneck Religion that brought it into being.

Clancy: You seem to speak of "Redneck Religion" in almost positive terms. Isn't this a step backward in the southern experience?

Campbell: Well, I seem to be getting that reputation. The syndicated columnist Paul Greenberg recently referred to me as the Aquinas of the Rednecks. While I would prefer to be the St. Francis of the Rednecks or the Pope John of the Rednecks, I was not insulted by his designation. Nor am I insulted that you would suggest that I speak of "Redneck" in positive terms. As you know, I have tried to do some writing on this subject and it is something in which I have more than a passing interest. That is from two reasons. That is my heritage, my history. I come from the poor-white group. I tried to live that down for a long time. Now I try to live it up. I think that a person is not whole until he or she can come to terms with his own history, whatever that history might be. But whatever it is, it is necessary to come to terms with it. The second reason is that I know the real racists in this country are not a few poor, pitiful people marching around a burning cross in a Carolina cow pasture. The racist enemy of us all is the system, those structures in which all of us who are white live and move and have our being and continue to profit from in one way or another every day of our lives. And the leaders, rulers, owners, managers of those structures are not the rednecks, but the university-educated, the sophisticated, nice gentlemen and ladies who make broad their phylacteries in the Cathedral (be it of Rome, Canterbury, Geneva, New York, or Nashville), know where the salad fork goes, have good taste in literature, music, and philosophy but continue to maintain a system wherein a very few whites own and run it all, while all blacks and most whites run none of it. Also, I am offended by the term "redneck." It is the same as "nigger." But if the term is going to be used, then count me in, call me one. And I'll deal with it as best I can, just as black people have had to deal with "nigger."

Clancy: In the past you have criticized liberal churchmen for selling out their religious birthright for "a piece of the social action," yet you demand that they witness to what they are. What kind of witness are you looking for?

Campbell: You have answered your question. Of course, I do not "demand" that they witness to what they are. The word is "implore," the same word used by St. Paul in II Corinthians 5. What he said was, "We implore you, *katallegate* to God!" The key to this is that it is the Greek imperative usage of the verb. Be reconciled. He did not say, "Try to become reconciled," but rather "Be reconciled"—"be what you already are" is what he was really saying. Earlier in the chapter he had said, "He has reconciled us men to himself through Christ." He has—past tense. It is over, it is already done. Well, I see that I will have to engage in a bit of horse-and-buggy exegeting to make the point. So let's back up a bit. In that chapter, St. Paul, in my judgment, summarized the Gospel in a fashion never done before or since. Earlier he had said that God has already reconciled, settled things, set things right between people and people and between people and God. And then he added a very crucial message when he said, "no longer holding man's misdeeds against him." (I have always assumed that that meant women too.) Now if our misdeeds are not held against us that means we are free. It means we do not have to do anything. We are not called upon to establish a Kingdom but to abide in one already established and to bid others to do the same. Just groove it, man. "And He enlisted us in this service of reconciliation." There's all the doctrine of the Church anyone needs. That's what the Church is—those who accept this enlistment. And all St. Paul called upon us to do is to live as if what God did in Christ is true. But our programs, schemes, strategies, next steps in this, that, or the other say that Paul is a liar—that God did not really reconcile us to one another and to Himself. I believe that He did. Therefore, if I am reconciled there is no such thing as nigger, redneck, Polack, Spic, Injun, Mick, Mackerelsnapper, Kluxer, etc., etc. To document that this is the case, Paul, in the same passage, said, "No longer do we judge anyone by worldly standards. Even though once we did [and we damn sure did] in our understanding of Christ, we do so now no longer." (That is the New English Bible translation I am quoting.) So. There you are. It is quite clear. If those categories do not exist—all those worldly standards, or human categories we place one another in—then the problem is solved. We just live by what has already been done for us. If I am reconciled to someone then I sure Lord ain't going to lynch him, don't care if he lives next door to me, goes to Mass in Jesuit Bend, goes to school with my children, marries my daughters. That is the radical word from St. Paul. If you know of a denominational social action program that goes quite that far let me know and I'll be glad to join it. Most I am familiar with are pablum, romantic nonsense. I recall something Thomas Merton wrote for our journal not too long before he died, "Bonhoeffer himself said it was an 'Anglo-Saxon failing' to imagine that the Church was supposed to have a ready answer for every social problem." And the point of Merton's observation was given in a later issue of that journal by another Catholic, this time a layman, John Howard Griffin, when he recalled that good Trappist's answer to the perennial question of oppressor to victim: "What can we, as Christians, do to help?" "Before you do a damned thing," Tom would reply, "just be what you say you are, a Christian; then no one will have to tell you what to do. You'll know."

Clancy: Let's change the subject.
Campbell: Okay by me.

Clancy: Is the preoccupation with Church in the South a valid expression of religious conviction or a substitute for the more complex urban experiences of the rest of the country?
Campbell: I don't know.

Clancy: You don't know? Well, I don't know how that will read in manuscript form but if you don't know, you don't know.
Campbell: Well, I don't know.

Clancy: Would you care to speculate?
Campbell: No.

Clancy: I understand the parallels you find between the alienation of the poor black and the poor white in the South. Are there any parallels in their expressions of religious belief?
Campbell: Oh, I think there are. In both groups religious expression is still largely a matter of feeling. And I must say I am inclined to agree with them. There is emotion expressed in each group. And, of course, we are beginning to see some of that in mainline Christianity as well. But I don't know how authentic it is. There is a difference between the strings and drums and horns of a Pentecostal religious service and what some of you, since Vatican II, are seeing as liturgical renewal, which is, generally—"And how many guitars did you have in the Mass yesterday, Father?" There is a difference between the fervor of a completely impromptu singing and shouting which might take place in a Holiness mountain brush arbor and the fingerpicking of a well-rehearsed, though still double-jointed, Dominican in the so-called Folk Mass. It is not folk unless it is from the folk, and I don't believe that what we are seeing in Catholic and many sophisticated Protestant circles is of the folk any more than—add any good reliable Catholic liturgical source.

Clancy: Would you then want us to go back to Latin in the Mass?

Campbell: My God, yes! Wouldn't everybody? But anyway, we were talking about the parallel expressions between the poor black and the sects of the poor whites in the South. There is the same crying out, agonizing, begging of Sweet Jesus for deliverance. And there is a similar social activism in both as well. The stereotype is that the religion of the sects is a "pie in the sky by and by" sort of passivity. That is not true. We don't have the time here, but I believe that I can document a good case that the record of the sects in actively opposing, or at least seeing as major moral issues, such things as poverty, racism, exploitation of labor, war, and even sexism is considerably better than mainline Protestantism or most Catholic groups.

Clancy: Why do you suppose that is?

Campbell: Well, it may be as simple as the sects not having as much to risk or lose as the more established institutions. You can rebuild a brush arbor a lot easier than you can rebuild a cathedral. Or it may be that God is choosing to work and speak through the sects today, or is judging us through the sects. He that hath ears to hear, let him hear!

Clancy: What is the future of religion in the southern experience?

Campbell: Certainly I don't know for sure. I suppose no one does. In the first place I'm always afraid to try to second-guess God. He's such a character, you know. In my judgment the established churches of America, what I call "Steepled Religion," stand precisely where the rich, young ruler who came to Jesus stood—rich, powerful. And good. No one ever, certainly not I, accused the Steeples of being bad. It is a good outfit and can generally be counted upon to meet its quota in any community drive, right up there with the Red Cross, the UGF, Boy Scouts, League of Women Voters, etc. And certainly it is powerful. And certainly it is very rich. Yet Jesus said to go and get rid of all that and then come back and they would talk about discipleship. To render ourselves powerless, poor, and therefore, in this culture at least, no longer good, would be, in my judgment, the most responsible thing we could do. I saw in the paper not long ago where one congregation paid just under two million dollars for an adjoining lot. It was not to be used as a parking lot, or to house the computer (oh, yes, a lot of Sunday School lesson material is now being planned by a computer), or to build a new Betty Crocker kitchen annex or skating rink or gym. It was not to be used at all. It was bought just because it was there and because they had the money. Now you might say that is caricature. But is it? I mean really. Don't most of us do the same thing though it might be on a much more modest scale? And all of it casting its physical shadow, to say nothing of its spiritual shadow, on vermin-infested slums, pimps, addicts, whores, drunks, bums, and the rest of the least of these that Jesus announced He had come to bring sight, comfort, good news, and freedom to. That has got to be blasphemy. Calling evil, good. And good, evil. But anyway, what is the future of it all? I imagine the South will follow the rest of the country. The institutions will go on getting better, richer, and more powerful. Rome will move to Nashville. The Southern Baptist convention will send an ambassador to the Vatican and a Methodist Bishop will exchange diocese with a Catholic. And we'll call it progress and improved understanding and tolerance.

Clancy: You aren't against tolerance are you?
Campbell: Yes, I'm against tolerance. Who wants to be tolerated? I just want to be accepted as a Brother for whom Christ died.

Clancy: Let's try to end on a realistic note. You know that what you are suggesting as responsible is not going to be done. We are not going to sell all we own and give it to the poor. But let's suppose that we should. Just how responsible would that be? What would the future then be?
Campbell: It would be a lonely day, wouldn't it? Standing there naked and alone. No bells, no pews, no steeples, no air-conditioned sanctuary. I don't know what would happen if we drove down one morning for the seven o'clock Mass and there was nothing there: I suppose we would drive back home, have two or three cups of coffee and maybe a quick Bloody Mary, read the funnies, the sports page two or three times, and move on to the A&P ads. And maybe that afternoon we would meet down by the gas station, appoint a finance committee, and start all over again. But maybe also the lonely priest, now unemployed, would drop by. Maybe we would say, "Are you hungry, Father?" He would say, "Yes, if you have some bread would you please bring it out. And maybe a little wine." And maybe we would sit around this very table here in the kitchen and the Eucharist would be celebrated and we would know it was being celebrated in our very midst. And we would cry real loud and real long and hug and hang on to one another desperately and beg of each other: "What are we going to do? What are we going to do?" Like when somebody dies, you know. And maybe this would be followed by shouts of "Hallelujah! Hallelujah! The Lord God Omnipotent reigneth." Maybe the joy of it all would be overwhelming because maybe we

would be singing the psalms for the very first time in our lives. Maybe, Walter. I just don't know. But that would be realistic, wouldn't it?

Clancy: Is there anything you would like to close the interview with?
Campbell: Naw, I don't believe. Thank you anyway.

An Oral History with Will Davis Campbell, Christian Preacher

Orley B. Caudill / 1976

From the Mississippi Oral History Program, volume 157 (1980): 33–53, 86–100. Reprinted with permission of Dr. Louis Kyriakoudes, director, Center for Oral History and Cultural Heritage, University of Southern Mississippi.

Will D. Campbell: I think the reason why I chose Ole Miss was that this was home, you know. Really, when I went to the University of Mississippi, I've never been a very ambitious person as you can just look around and see, except that works both ways. It depends on what your goals are. I have had everything I want, I can't imagine anything I don't have, you know.

Orley B. Caudill: The going away to Yale to school now was not really a breaking with Mississippi; it was just getting an education?
Campbell: I didn't think it was. I didn't think it was, though so many of these things are self-defeating, as I'm trying to show that what we call progress may be regression.

I went off to Yale because it had been so instilled in me, "go and get that education, that's the key, get that." So that I could be the best, the most able minister to the people. I never rejected Mississippi. Never even during my sort of pseudo-sophistication period. I always had very strong emotional ties.

You can't grow up in that atmosphere and environment and not, I think, have that as long as you live. Even in your denying of it is affirming it.

Caudill: That's right. The denying of it is trying to improve on something that is dear to you, but you recognize the faults of it.
Campbell: Yes. So, I always intended on going back there but the very education that I thought was going to prepare me to best minister to, quote, "my people" is the thing that cut me off from it.

You know, when they said, when I would come back, you know, "He doesn't preach like he used to, you know. He doesn't have the same fervor," and they were right. I'd had something educated out of me.

Now, you can make the point that you've got something educated into you, too. That's true, but I wasn't the boy they had sent off, you know. They could see that, consequently I'm sure I could never have got a pastorate in Mississippi unless I had gone to Louisiana, you know, and been a very good boy, and finally lived that down.

They say, "Well, yes he went off up there and got some of that education, but he's the prodigal come back home." But I assumed that in a college situation, number one, I would be free, and also I would be home, though Oxford, Mississippi is, I guess, two hundred and fifty miles from Amite County; it was still Mississippi. When I went there, I intended to spend the rest of my life there. I never intended to move again; well, I lasted two and a half years. Which I think was somewhat of an accomplishment in that time.

Caudill: How long had you been there before you began to realize that your time would be rather short?
Campbell: Not long.

Caudill: Let's see. What was the chancellor? Was it Porter Fortune?
Campbell: No. J. D. Williams.

Caudill: J. D. Williams?
Campbell: Another good man. When I speak harshly of institutions, I don't mean to speak harshly of individuals or the ones who are involved in them. Chancellor Williams saw his role, his vocation, his call, his job—everything—as protecting the University of Mississippi and seeing that it survived. So that every time I got into trouble, this is where it always came down: "Look, you know, I don't blame you, Chancellor; I would be doing exactly what you're doing if I were in your seat, but I'm not in your seat. I am in another seat. I have a different view; I don't have any feeling about this institution. I'm not trying to tear it down. I'm not trying to prop it up. It's irrelevant. It doesn't matter." I believe that about all institutions, beginning with the structure of the steeple of the institutional church, which is where I think Christianity, or its organization, got off the track. The peace and harmony within the fellowship is considered the desirable norm. The goal of what it means to be a Christian is to be active in a fellowship, in an organization of harmony and peace.

Caudill: But on the other hand Chancellor Williams just by virtue—of course he undoubtedly believed it also, but that really was his role, wasn't it? Or was it?

Campbell: It was his role. Of course, it was his role. I never argued with him about that. The only argument I ever had is "don't try to press me into that channel. That is not where I fit."

I think, and I believe this, that it would have been a healthy thing for me to have been free to be the hell raiser and to exercise a prophetic, for lack of better term, ministry there. My message to the people that I remained in communication with in deep Mississippi during that very, very difficult period was that, "Look, what I'm working for, what I'm trying to do, will mean that desegregation of your public schools will be slower in coming." Nobody was after Mississippi in 1954, they weren't even thinking about Mississippi. But then when the resistance became so strong, then it was an inevitable course.

Caudill: They brought this upon themselves, in other words?

Campbell: Right. There's no question that they brought it upon themselves. Now that's not to say that the schools in Mississippi would not have been finally desegregated; they would have been. That era was gone, that era was over, but when I went to the University of Mississippi in 1954, my public position was "look, if we all agree that this decision was just, right, and necessary, it would still take ten to fifteen years to just work out the logistics of it," but that was too much, you know. We're not talking about ifs, we're talking about never. Well, you don't talk about never, I don't care what the subject is, what the circumstances.

Caudill: No, that's right. Never is just too long.

Campbell: That's too long. That's too long. And, of course, the chancellor saw that. When I went there, when I was interviewed for that job, this barely came up, but the chancellor told me, "I had some of the leading students in our home the other night, fifty or seventy-five editors, fraternity presidents, et cetera, and went around the room. 'Who would object if we could find some well qualified'—then again the term that always offended me from a Christian point of view, that only qualified were human or have some rights—'how many of you would object to bringing say someone into the graduate school of education'"—they always somehow want to start in education—and as I recall, no one objected, you know.

And this campus paper, the year that I went there, did a poll and it was an overwhelming majority that would have favored desegregation of the university at all levels.

Caudill: Is that right? They voted that? I didn't know that.
Campbell: Yes, in the poll; now in one year that had completely reversed. I don't remember if it was an eighty-twenty, but whatever it was, it had totally reversed.

Caudill: Do you suppose the reality was the reason for the reversal?
Campbell: Well, the social pressures. The organizing of the White Citizens Council was without a doubt the most influential thing. I was at the University of Mississippi when Judge Tom Brady went over to, I believe it was Greenwood, when he gave the first address, which later became Black Monday, which later became one of the strongest social movements this country has ever seen. The most influential and powerful because it was concerned with an area that was filled with so much emotional intensity, and so much economics, and the whole social pattern. It was an extremely significant movement, and reached into every part of this country.

Caudill: I didn't realize that it would be so strong, say in the Northwest.
Campbell: As an organization, certainly it wasn't strong but the thinking was there. I think the truth is that this country—and I hope by now we've long since quit thinking in terms of North and South. That's something I never took very seriously because I've lived in the North, but the degree of Negrophobia that has plagued this country from the very beginning has never really been faced up to.

We've either said "it's the South" or "it's Mississippi" or "it's a few states in the South" or "it's south Boston" or it's somewhere.

Now we're saying "it's the rednecks," you know. "It's not Westchester County, it's the rednecks." That's not accurate. It's operative at every level, in every group, and I think until we really do face up to it and at least try to diagnose the malady, we're never going to.

We haven't really moved toward any kind of cure to the problem of race in America. Of course, today if you still want to talk about race relations they say, "Ahh—he's just an old soldier; he can't quite give up the fight, you know. He's nostalgic; he's thinking about the old movement, how they used to march across the Selma bridge." Again—"he'll be all right."

Caudill: What were the major confrontations that you had at Ole Miss? Now where did you begin to get into difficulties with the administration there?

Campbell: Well, the first dramatic confrontation was—I had been there a short while when I read in the paper about a farm—it was called "a communal farm," but it really was not a communal farm—in Holmes County, called Providence Farm, which had been started in the thirties by a young group of churchmen who had come under the influence of Sherwood Eddy, Kirby Page, and Reinhold Niebuhr, and others. Probably their political orientation was socialist, but they went in there and set up this farm. One of them a doctor, one a nurse and they ran a clinic primarily for blacks, though they didn't exclude anybody.

The majority of the poor populace was black and they organized credit unions, co-ops. They were missionaries, you know, really.

After the White Citizens Council was organized, and things began to get really tense, they had been there for twenty-odd years, you know. Nobody had paid any great attention to them. They knew they were there, Eugene Cox and Doctor Minter. They were active in their local churches, and schools, PTA and so on and were not really violating any of the segregation patterns.

They didn't have white and colored signs over the waiting room but people knew that a white should go to this room and everybody else go in here.

But there was an incident where—this was right after the Emmett Till case—one of the children, white girls on the farm, was waiting for a school bus one morning and an old flatbed truck passed. It had three or four black kids in the back, and like kids would do, they were hollering off the truck and she got frightened, no doubt because of all the Bryant-Milam trial and the Emmett Till case and all of the publicity.

She was crying when the school bus driver came along and the woman asked her what she was crying about and she didn't want to tell her. Finally she said that "one of those colored kids hollered at her."

The driver said, "Well, I want you to tell the principal as soon as you get to school." The little girl didn't want to do it, so she said, "If you don't tell her, I'm going to tell her."

Well, the upshot was the principal called the DA, or the sheriff, one, and they picked up this boy, black kid, who was alleged to have done the hollering, They questioned him for two hours with a tape recorder, and there was a meeting convened, a mass meeting, at the schoolhouse in Tchula where this tape was played. It was real innocuous for the most part, they were obviously trying to get him to admit to something. The black kid had lived on the farm also at one time.

"Did you ever see Negroes and whites swimming together?" "Yes sir." Well, he spoke the truth, but what he had seen was the Minters and the Coxes, the Cox woman was a nurse, the Minter was the doctor; the Cox man ran the big general store, organized the federal credit unions, the co-ops, and so forth. They had small children; they had a big blown-out part of a creek bed there which was dangerous, so they had bought the maid a bathing suit to watch the kids, and she would get out there and hold the little kids—that was the integrated swimming.

"Well, do you ever have meetings?" "Yes sir."

"What does Mr. Cox talk about?" "He talk about Jesus and trees"— and Gene couldn't remember what in the world that was about for a long time. Finally he remembered at one time showing a reforestation film and they would always start these meetings with prayer, and end them with benediction.

So this little kid, this again—about whether people listen to your speeches or not. That made an impression, planting trees, you know, and he remembered Jesus got in somehow. "They talked about Jesus and the trees."

Well, this infuriated this group and there were already by then lots of rumors around.

I read about this and decided of course I had to go down there and get into it. So I went down there and found them under a state of siege, actually. That's the only word to describe it; they didn't know me and they weren't coming out. There was another man with me, a guest speaker, named Dr. McCloud Bryan, who was then teaching at a little Baptist college in Georgia, Mercer University.

My style was to be as innocuous appearing as possible. But his—every little thing had a built-in mechanism to trigger some kind of bomb. So they would assume "what would be safer than a philosophy professor from a Baptist college in Georgia." Though, when he got there, of course, he just dropped bombs all over the place! Quoting Faulkner and quoting Hodding Carter and quoting Billy Graham, their enemies and their friends, you know.

So he went with me and they knew him so they came out and we talked about the story. There was a roadblock so that the black patients couldn't get to the clinic. They were having no practice; the telephone lines had been cut. Every night there was a little group down at the road to keep anybody from coming in or out. It was really something I had never experienced before.

Well I said—I was just this young and foolish prophet, and "hell, this is the United States of America; it's not Nazi Germany and I done fought three years of my life, and I don't have to live like this. I'm going to drive my car right through." There was another road around, they had told me, that could get me out.

By then this posse comitatus had come and informed them to leave the county, you know. "If you don't, we can't assume responsibility for what's going to happen to you." At that point they couldn't leave. My God, that was their life. They had lived there for twenty years. But they did eventually leave.

They simply stopped my car, didn't say anything to me, shined a big flashlight in my eyes, went around and got the license plate number. The next day, the rumors were flying all over the campus, you know. The Chancellor wants to see Will Campbell. Well, I was just playing it real cool and sure enough, pretty early in the morning the vice-chancellor, I believe, who was Mr. Hugh Clegg—

Caudill: Clegg?

Campbell: Clegg called and said, "I want to see you and I'll call you again later." Now this may be a little rusty, you know. I'm not positive that it was Mr. Clegg. The one who eventually came to see me was the provost, Dean Alton Bryant, a good man, who was on my board. Though I worked for the state, I used to tell the students when they moved in on me, "Look, if you want to get rid of me, all you have to do is challenge the constitutionality of this chair I'm sitting in. It's just as unconstitutional as it can be, for the state of Mississippi has got no business paying ministers."

Well they didn't want to do that because there had always been a chaplain. You know, Dean Guest was the most beloved man in the history of the school and he had that job, and it was state-church, you know, and too good a thing to fight. You don't want to do that.

Finally Dean Bryant, about five o'clock in the afternoon, came over. He said, "I'm going to be very candid with you. The state senator from Holmes County was on the campus this morning and apparently the sheriff of Holmes County had called the sheriff of Lafayette County and had got the license number, who it was, and said he wants to know what the hell one of our men was doing in Holmes County last night."

He said, "We don't want you to think we're scared. We don't want you to think we're critical, but we've got to give them an answer." So I said, "All right."

This was my cue. We've got to give them an answer, and here's the answer: I launched into this sophonic tirade. "Yes, I was in Holmes County, and I'll tell you what I was doing there. I was down there visiting some Christian missionaries." I told them the story of the history of that farm and what they were doing. One set of the parents had been Presbyterian ministers in Burma, I believe, and another set of parents had been missionaries in China, chased out by communists and all that business. It was far from what they were being accused of, which was being communist. They had fought the communists when it was costly to fight the communists in the revolution in China, their parents did.

"Tell them, that not only was I there but I'm going back Sunday afternoon." This was like Friday and I said, "Dean, I'll be glad if you will go with me. Now you say you're not scared and you're not critical. Well, I'm scared to think that fascism has reached the state in the United States of America where a Christian can't drive his car across the county line to see some of his brothers and sisters without his name, his license number noted, his boss called, for what purpose other than to intimidate him into not returning. Now that scares me."

So Dean Bryant said he was quite aware of what I was saying, but again, with these institutional responsibilities, he said, "I guess maybe the time comes when you just can't do any educating. You just have to wait."

I said, "Well, maybe so but the time never comes when it's wise to call the fireman when the fire's out, or when the house has burned down. Then we can talk or I can sermonize some about the threat of the White Citizens Council to our education."

He said, "You will agree, Will, that this University is the one place of hope in the state"— Mississippi Southern and Mississippi State obviously didn't count. Ole Miss—and true, Ole Miss at that time was producing the rulers, the legislators, and the lawyers and so on. "And," he said, "if we get in any kind of trouble, we've got a moss-back old governor down there, a legislature down there, that will close this place up. I know, I lived through it with Bilbo."

Well, I was familiar with that, when he had gotten rid of Chancellor Hume and virtually the entire faculty. I was aware of that.

So that was the first. That was the first of several confrontations and altercations that led to my rather early demise.

Caudill: Did you finally resign or did you reach a mutual understanding?

Campbell: I resigned. I could have remained through the contract year, I'm quite sure. I still had some support following that, almost paralleling that incident which continued of course to make ripples around the state.

Though I'm not very good at an awful lot of things, but one thing I was good at—maybe just because I was a coward—but I was good at staying out of the press, and I saw that very early.

All the time I worked for the National Council of Churches in race relations, at the time the riots were going on, the time that the kids at school were being dynamited, I was at all those places, and I just never got in the press.

I'm a little bit proud about that because it would have been so easy to have become a folk hero for a short period of time.

Caudill: Yes, there are some who came out of the war movement for instance, I think, to a substantial extent. . . . This one confrontation, how was that settled?
Campbell: Oh, there was never any settlement to it.
[. . .]

Caudill: You are quoted in both the book and in one of the articles here as, I don't recall the exact quotation but "carrying the bedpans out for the Klansmen" as one means of, I guess, ministering for them.
Campbell: Yes, all that means is that this has got to be a pastoral relationship.

Caudill: This is what you really are going to do with all of your life is in some means be a pastor?
Campbell: Yes, right. Right. Yes. I go around to meet with these groups sometimes, and they want to talk right off about your work with the Ku Klux Klan. "Well, I don't have any work with the Ku Klux Klan." "Well, we read so and so where you do." "Well, I know, yeah, I do sometimes have funerals or weddings." I see nothing incongruous about this. It is so very elementary that the scriptural admonition about release to the captives . . . When was I imprisoned? It doesn't say unless you're a member of the Ku Klux Klan, or unless you are a black militant—it just says sick people, or people who are in prison. I realize that because of the lines drawn in the culture there is a certain romance and drama about this, but I don't think I intended it to be. I didn't deliberately go out and say, "I am going to have a ministry to the Ku Klux Klan," as the Ku Klux Klan.

Now, I do admit to wanting to get to know a number of these people in order to be able to interpret to the larger community a part of the tragedy, and to be able to say with some authority, "Look, the problem of race in America is not invested in a pathetic little group of folks marching around and burning crosses in a Carolina or Mississippi cow pasture. That's not the enemy." I think I can make a case that again university as university teaches, fosters, sponsors, carries out more violence in one semester than the Ku Klux Klan has throughout its history, and has more institutional racism than the Ku Klux Klan has. Now then, they may be more prejudiced; they may be more bigoted than the "children of light." But they're not more racist. Racism is the structures, the system in which we are all bound up. So I'm a racist; you're a racist just by this purely skin disease called whiteness. We can't help it. It doesn't mean we're bigots. It doesn't even mean we're prejudiced. But it does mean that we live within these structures where by the accident of birth you can be governor of Mississippi; no black person yet can be. President of the United States, I could have been president of the Southern Baptist Convention, pastor of the First Baptist Church in Atlanta, if my nervous system ran in that direction. So that makes me a racist. It doesn't make me a bigot.

And going back to my friend at Harvard University, we're all basically of a Klan mentality when it comes to our own structures and our own institutions. I learned a great lesson from a guy that I referred to as head of the Maoist wing of the Ku Klux Klan in North Carolina, because he considered the United Klans too moderate; there were divisions. I asked him one night what the Ku Klux Klan stood for. His wife was there and we had been going through a lot of stuff together and quick as a wink, he said, "We stand for peace and harmony and freedom." Well, I wasn't quite ready for that, you know.

Caudill: For peace, harmony, and freedom! [laughter]
Campbell: It wasn't my notion of the Klan. And of course being educated, and he uneducated, I figured, well I can handle this situation. I'll play his little Socratic fun game with him, and asked a very profound question, "And what do you mean by peace and harmony and freedom?" He said, "Well, I mean the same thing you mean. They're in the dictionary. If you don't know what the words mean, go look them up." Well, okay, in other words you define the words. Yeah, and in effect—this was a fairly drawn out conversation—who defines the words you use? When you use a word, it's your word. In other words all language is symbol—that and nothing more. Okay, you stand for peace and harmony and freedom; you define the words. Then what are the means you are willing to use: murder, torture, intimidation, burning, looting, guerilla warfare, whatever, you know. Well, I thought, "Okay, I won." And then after this long pause, he said, "Now, preacher, you tell me what the hell we're doing over here in Veet Nam." Then I saw who won—that

we're a nation of Kluxers. We stood for peace and harmony and freedom; we defined the words, and it didn't take some pathetic little character like William Calley to prove it.

Caudill: Who was it, Mr. Dooley, that said, "The words mean precisely what I want them to mean and nothing more and nothing less"?
Campbell: Gore said that.

Caudill: How do you minister? You have mentioned that you marry people without the license. Is that legal?
Campbell: I don't know and don't care. What is the difference?

Caudill: In some states I would assume that people would be in jeopardy of some law, like bigamous cohabitation, or unbigamous cohabitation, or something like that.
Campbell: They may be. They may be, but again that is Caesar's realm. Now if they have a license, which they generally do, I sign it. I really am not sure that I ought to say, "Now if you want to get married, I'll marry you. Then if you want to have a legal contract to give one another the right to sue the other party, you can only do that in another Caesar's courts, before another of his agents; you can't come to me for that."

Caudill: I hadn't really thought about that, but that really is the basis for the legal marriage.
Campbell: Of course, it is.

Caudill: Legal contract, isn't it.
Campbell: Of course, it is. Now I'll marry you and then I have a friend down here named Buell Agee and for five dollars—I don't charge you anything for my services, but for five dollars—he will sign, he'll execute your contract. That's what I am convinced I ought to do, I think, the social pressures are such. But this is one small way in which I think it could be dramatized that there is a difference between law and grace, between the state and the church. As it now stands for the most part, there is no distinction really, civil religion. "The good Christian is the good citizen." He may be or he may not be.

Caudill: Yes, in fact many good Christians are not very good Christians.
Campbell: Yes. Yes.

Caudill: That really is one of your arguments too, isn't it?
Campbell: Sure.

Caudill: Now you talk about the institutions. What kind of a society would you like to see, if you had your druthers, to accomplish the kind of world that you would like to see exist?
Campbell: Now, that's the wrong question. I mean it's a question I can't deal with, or won't deal with, because the minute you begin to deal with that question, you're saying "I think that I can do better than the other institutions. I think I can set up better institutions." I can't.

Caudill: Just the minute you start doing it, it institutionalizes it.
Campbell: Yes, the minute you say that. I'm not trying to set up; I don't find anything in the New Testament faith, and very little in the Old Testament, but certainly the New Testament, that has the slightest concern with any kind of society, with any civilization. It's not concerned, you know. Yes, there are points in there that talk about "being obedient to the civil powers" and so on. Well, I do that. There is that "render unto Caesar the things that are Caesar's," indicating that at least something is of Caesar. I'm quite willing to acknowledge that and even—which probably, may be one of my greatest sins—to participate in it, like the signing of the marriage agreement, a document, a legal contract.

Caudill: Well, you pay your taxes, too.
Campbell: I pay my taxes. Yes, a number of things. But you pretend as if, because there is that scripture, "give to Caesar what is Caesar's," then you just let him rule, run everything, that's to give him what is not his and what in many cases he is not even asking for. This is what troubles me with a awful lot of Christian people and Christian institutions. You know, go right here and here's some more and here's something else you forget about. We want to help you with this, too. We want to be your chaplains, is what it comes down to. We want a piece of the action. So, I would no more run for Congress as a minister and say, "What we need to do is get more Christian people in politics." That's absolute nonsense, to me. If I wanted to be a congressman and thought I could be elected, it's a good job. Go out there and run for it, but it doesn't have anything to do with any Christian vocation. How can you be a Christian congressman? What do you do? Say prayers on the floor of the House every day?

Caudill: It's possible: One of the articles calls you almost an anarchist.
Campbell: I know that.

Caudill: Which means that you would like to see governmental institutions abolished.
Campbell: Yes, but see, what the article calls me and what I really think is two totally different things. I'm not a Christian anarchist, and that's the term that is used by some people, friends and critics, who are friendly critics, to sort of categorize me, because there is no such thing as a Christian anarchist, because anarchy is a political arrangement. I am not an anarchist—

Caudill: And a Christian has nothing to do with it?
Campbell: I am not a non-anarchist.

Caudill: What I was really trying to ask a moment ago is, if I can articulate it, what kind of a society would you like to see?
Campbell: [Laughter] You articulated very well. I have no idea. That's not my concern. I'm not trying to create any kind of society. I am trying to talk in terms of Christian response wherever one may be, and whatever society. This is where Karl Barth was so badly misunderstood during the Nazi period when he said of the Nazis, "The Christian response is to pretend that they are not there, they don't exist." A lot of people read that as "the old man is saying so what if there are seven million Jews being burned, and incinerated; and lamp shades made out of their skin, and soap out of their flesh. Just pretend it's not happening."

That's not what he was saying at all. He was saying that your response, what you do as a Christian, has got to be the same whether or not he is going to cut your head off or whether there is someone out there who is going to pin a medal on you. That's not your concern.

But the minute you say, "Well, I want this kind of society," then inevitably I'm going to want to be king of that society because I'm the only one who knows what kind of society we ought to have, so obviously I ought to be the one running it. Well, I would never say that. God knows, I wouldn't know how to do any better than Dick Nixon or Jerry Ford or Franklin Roosevelt or any of the others.

I can't improve on these institutional structures. I think that public schools in this country are very, very repressive and evil. If somebody says, "Well, can you set up a better system for us?" and I would say, "No, I couldn't do that, I don't know how."

Somebody said, "Well, you're very critical of that steeple; you call your-self a steeple dropout, you don't go to the sacred service anymore. Why don't you establish a better church." Well, I could have done that, you know. I know that. We have a guest house here, a sort of a mini folk school back there in the fields, just a small cottage, you know, but a lot of things go on, seminars or prayers. Every once in a while some of the neighbors have been in on this and sometimes we might have a service, like we had when the Catholic priest who was gunned down with Jonathan Daniels, in Lowndes County, came here for part of his later recuperation period. He would say mass up there.

Some of the neighbors and friends around used to come, they would say, "Well, this was nice. None of us go to church. We have the facilities here, why don't we meet every Sunday." Very simple, because to do that is to start another institution.

Caudill: Yes, you've got an institution meeting every Sunday, haven't you?
Campbell: Pretty soon, we're going to be arguing about whether we have communion with Welch's grape juice or Mogen David wine, and pretty soon I'm going to want to be the pastor because I have title to the house.

Caudill: Let me ask in a different vein—I'm going in a different direction now. You write and you have a substantial education. How much of your time do you spend now in reading and preparing? How do you really spend your time, say from week to week now?
Campbell: Well, I don't do the same thing twice very often, so that's a hard question to answer. As far as reading, I am not a reader; I am not one of the new breed who takes pride in the fact that I don't read anything anymore. It's just that I never did learn to read really; I'm almost a lip-finger reader, and consequently I don't really have time to read. I read the newspapers. I read some magazines or parts of them. It would be difficult to say. Well, last week for example—I have a short attention span. Last week I had to do two funerals, both of them in Louisiana, and from there I went to the University of Tennessee to give two addresses—as we formally call them—to the grad-uating seniors at the UT School of Social Work to try to get their re-entry into the world. When I got back here, there was a group here from Texas who stayed in the guest house and we talked, you know. Some of them have got some problems. A young man who is in prison, and he is coming up for probation hearing. It takes some time to try to set this up with the lawyers, and the witnesses, and try to get him a job if he gets out and so on. That took some time. We have a little farm here, I spent some time working on it,

which is really nothing more than my golf. I like to do it; it's my recreation. It just happens to be edible; can't eat golf balls because they wouldn't be very tasty. [laughter].

Caudill: You get a better product out of it at least.

Campbell: This week there's a young fellow here from Georgia, who will stay with us all week. I'll spend some time with him. I talk to you. Sunday I will leave to go to Chicago for two weeks with the National Association of College and University Chaplains, or whatever that's called—a workshop lecturing situation. I want to spend some time on a magazine we publish. I do some writing, but not a great deal. So it's a very, very diversified kind of thing.

Caudill: Do you have to structure your time fairly precisely?

Campbell: I don't. That's not to say I shouldn't. I'm just not a very disciplined person. I'm not an organized person.

Caudill: What do you like to do for enjoyment?

Campbell: Oh, I enjoy it all. I don't know what people are talking about today when they say they're bored. Or when they ask, "Tell us what we can do in race relations" or in anything, because if somebody has got to ask that question, generally they don't want to know. I know that I can sit right here in this valley and never go out except when situations would take me out, and have a full time ministry, of just people in this community.

Caudill: Now do you mean in a church or they come in to visit?

Campbell: No, just the people that we know around here. There's a black man who lives over here who is ninety years old, we've got to check on him and to see if he's got some coal or whatever, you know. Here's a couple living over here and have got two small children and are scared to death because the daughters are going to do exactly what they did when they were that age. Here's one on across there, they start drinking beer at seven o'clock in the morning, and we know damn well they're going to be serious alcoholics in a very few years.

These are all people who want something. They're not turning you away; they are very appreciative of anything whether you read the riot act to them or whatever. There is this kid with mother and father in the work house, his grandfather was a good friend of mine. We do what we can, you know; now that's not to say that is the ministry I have, because I neglect those people for the most part.

Caudill: When you make a speech like over at University of Tennessee, do you charge honorariums occasionally?

Campbell: No. I have never done that, and it's not that I'm against money. And it's not that I don't need it; it's just that I think that I know that there have been a few periods in my life that I could have capitalized and exploited and got on the lecture circuit with an agent, but right off—and there is nothing really heroic in this—right off that agent is going to package you, because he's got a percentage of the cut, and he's going to be sending you here and there, whether that's where you need to be or want to be, or not. It's just not the kind of structured thing I want to go into. I may someday have to do that, I don't know.

Caudill: Yes, you could have done it after the civil rights violent period ended.

Campbell: Yes, and the whole thing when the HUAC [House Un-American Activities Committee] was after the Klan and all there were those which were very dramatic kind of, dramatic to some people, involvements there. I could have gone on the circuit with some of that. There are various and sundry packages that could be tied up, but I really think it's more important to sort of hang loose, so that if somebody calls and wants you to come that if you don't feel that you have anything to say, that cup of dishwater now. I get tired sometimes because a lot of people have got to have an out-of-town speaker from time to time, so it doesn't really matter much what you do. "Here's some guy with a little color that you can get a good press release out about him." I try to avoid those things—what does it mean, you know. I do accept some very, very frankly. I wouldn't go into it two weeks any more unless it's something pretty close to a personal thing, unless they were going to pay me something for it, like going to this Chicago thing. I think that I will be able to make some contribution. I also think I'll learn something. These are fellows, younger than myself, or of a different orientation, we'll knock heads, and carry on. I think I will come out of it intellectually profiting. And I think that I will be able to say some things maybe that they hadn't thought of before—things that I think they ought to learn. But even so, I imagine I wouldn't have done it if they hadn't said there would be a little stipend.

Caudill: Well, it helps, doesn't it?

Campbell: Yes.

Caudill: Do you regard yourself—you really are an individualist is what you're saying, is it?

Campbell: Well, I'm not saying anything.

Caudill: That's what they're saying, whoever they are?

Campbell: Well, I'm not going to say that either way. I think if somebody asked me, "What are you trying to do?" I am trying to survive as a human being and not as some technological robot, a programmed computer type of anything. Now if that makes for an individualist, then that's all right. But I think whatever Jesus meant—I think I know what he meant—when he talked in terms of if you want to find your life, you lose it. I think that means various and sundry things. I think what he was talking about was, if you want to find out who you are, forget it. All this questioning who am I?—or what am I?—generally lands you on the analyst's couch. I don't know who I am and I don't care, don't want to know, and I may not like me. As it is, I get along fairly well.

Caudill: Yes. I agree. Who do you count—now this may not be a very good question but you've known a lot of people who are prominent, among them blacks and whites. Stokely Carmichael. Did you know Martin Luther King well?

Campbell: Yes, I knew him quite well. I was not of course as close to him as the blacks, like Andy Young and others, who were close in the movement with him. I knew him pretty well.

Caudill: Who would you consider—I'm not sure how to ask this. Of the people with whom you worked, for their efforts, for whom would you have the highest regard?

Campbell: Oh, I wouldn't begin to—I wouldn't begin—to answer that. With my understanding of the nature of man, or of humanity, I really think you can't draw any sharp distinctions, you know. Really, ultimately, we—every one of us is just one more marine, you know. There's not really anything special about any one of us, except that there is something special about us all. Did you ever hear of the name P. D. East?

Caudill: P. D. East?

Campbell: P. D. East ran, for a number of years, *The Petal Paper*—across the river from Hattiesburg.

Caudill: Yes. Yes.

Campbell: He got into some trouble. He was a sort of character, you know. He was sort of an iconoclastic, bombastic guy who latched on to me, or we sort of latched on to one another when I was at Ole Miss. He was a sometime friend of Faulkner's. He got involved in a little thing called the

Southern Reposure, sort of an underground newspaper out of Ole Miss. Some students started it, but he picked it up for a while; it never amounted to much. P. D. was very critical of the church, which he equated with the Christian faith. I used to argue with him, and tell him he didn't know what he was talking about, which most of the time he didn't when he was talking about religion. He asked me one time, "What is Christianity? I'm not too bright, but maybe if you try to explain it, I might kind of get a little handle on it." I said, "Well, all men are bastards but God loves us anyway." So when my friend Jonathan Daniels was killed down in Lowndes County, Alabama, I happened to be down at P. D.'s house, with my brother who was still living then, and they were both sort of between wives and they were holed up down at Fairhope, Alabama. I was visibly upset by this and P. D. said, "Will, what do you think Mr. Jesus thinks about all this?" I said, "I imagine he's kind of agonizing over it."

He said, "Well, how does that definition of yours of the Christian faith hold up in this kind of situation?" And I had long since forgotten the occasion. "I don't remember what you mean." "You know, what you said, the definition of Christianity is 'all men are bastards but God loves us anyway.' Let me ask you, was Jonathan Daniel a bastard?" Well, here was a young man twenty-three years old, good fellow, sweet gentle person. That wasn't an easy question, but I knew I was in a trap, you know. Either way I went I was in trouble. "Just yes or no. Was he a bastard?" "Well, yes, I guess so." "Okay. Was Thomas Coleman a bastard?" That's the one who killed him. "Why, yeah. Yeah. He's a bastard." He said, "Which one of these bastards do you think God loves most?" That's a pretty profound question and I hedged, you know. "Well, God loves the sinner and not the sin." He waved his hand in a fashion of negation. "I don't want to hear about that. I don't know what you're talking about. Just yes or no. Which one? Just name one. Which one of these two bastards? Does God love John, that little bastard Jonathan Daniel, lying down there in that morgue more than he loves Thomas Coleman, the bastard sitting in his own jail over there in Lowndes County? Which one of them does he love the most? You said that God loves us all. We're all bastards and God loves us anyway. Which one does he love the most?" I said, "Well, I'll tell you. I want to revise that definition. We're all bastards, but you've got to be the biggest bastard of all because you're about to make a Christian out of me and damn if I think I can stand it." Which he thought was hilarious, because he never thought of himself as a Christian proselytizer. So in that understanding, I wouldn't try to rate or rank anybody.

Caudill: Let me restate it just a little bit. Martin Luther King was very influential, and Stokely Carmichael sort of flashed across the sky for a period of time. Who would have been the more influential people that you came into contact with in the civil rights movement? Or did you more or less come into contact with most of them?

Campbell: Well, I came into contact with most of them, I suppose. I don't think there's any question that King, as a symbol, was probably the most influential person in the whole civil rights movement. He was, from the early days, the symbol but I think "symbol" is the word here. It does not mean that he was necessarily more committed, or braver, or stronger, you know. If you do that, what are you going to do with Mrs. Rosa Parks, who sort of triggered the thing by refusing to move to the back of the bus? What are you going to do about the Pullman porter, Mr. Nixon, who was sort of the brains behind it? What are you going to do with Glenn Smiley, who was probably the forming influence on King to adopt the Gandhian nonviolent position? This was all alien to King's thinking. What are you going to do—

Caudill: He just happened to be the instrument then—in which a lot of currents converged?

Campbell: Oh, sure. In this, I am not going to take anything away from him at all. I just say he wasn't alone.

Caudill: And he was sharp enough to play the role, wasn't he?

Campbell: Paul talked about the earthen vessels and things can happen through us and that after all was said and done, we are pots. Earthen vessels and clay pots in all of this.

Caudill: I think I've only got about one other question to ask you, then I'd like to ask you if there's something that we've gone away from before you got a chance to discuss it, or any thoughts that you'd like to express. This is probably not possible, but if you were able to project yourself back to your ordination day at the age of seventeen, and looking forward to where you are today, are you where you would like to have been? Have you travelled the road to reach the point that you would like to have reached?

Campbell: Well, of course, that is a very difficult question to deal with. I think I'm more nearly in harmony and at peace with that rite, r-i-t-e, than at some other periods of my lifetime. I think that what the people there that day, when my grandfather—I was kneeling down there—put his arthritic, bony, calloused hands, fingers, on my head and stood there, as if he were waiting for all the resources and power in his own body to flow into mine, and what they had to do was to make me a preacher, and if I had any self-image today, that's what it is, with all the stigma and derogatory connotations that a lot of people place on that term. I don't happen to share that. I wear the distinction with pride. I know that I'm not what many people in the institutional church would call a preacher. They say "you don't have a church, how can you be a preacher?" All I can say to that is they must not read the New Testament very closely and all that.

That passage, those couple of pages I read earlier about women, we are going to publish that, which I am directing pretty much at the Episcopalians, because their two big issues at their convention this year is ordination of women and rewriting the prayer book. I'm entitling it, it's part of a larger manuscript, I'm entitling that anecdote, that article, "Retiring Twelve Women Priests Rework the Prayer Book!" If I know what a priest is, someone who participates in a service, a litany, someone who supports others and holds them up and celebrates life and expresses hope and resurrection, and someone who is a teacher; they obviously were teachers. If I remember this forty years later or longer—if I myself, sitting here in this small cabin writing about that—they very obviously were teachers. They were priests, you know. It doesn't make any difference whether somebody votes on them, or what the General Convention of the Episcopal Church does; they're priests. God raises up His own priests, so what the culture may call a preacher, yes, I don't fit into that stereotype; I don't want to. But my understanding of preacher, I think; most of the people who were involved in that, only one of whom is still living, that's my own father, they would have asked a lot of questions along the way and raised a lot of eyebrows, most of them. Some of them wouldn't but my father certainly would, maybe at every point along the way. But I think overall they would say, "Yeah, I think the old boy is pretty much being faithful to what we had in mind for him to do when we turned him loose out there in the world.

Caudill: There's a certain amount of comfort in that.
Campbell: Well, again that's the sort of thing I don't like to dwell on. That's not the same as saying the sort of people that are in my life, because there are not any good boys. We will close this up with I'm a bastard, too. "I am a bastard." [laughter]

Caudill: Well, let me thank you for taking so much of your day and I do apologize for arriving early this morning. I'd like to suggest that when we

get a manuscript which will be several months, there may be some aspects of it that might be worth sitting down again sometime.
Campbell: Yes. Okay.

Caudill: On behalf of the university, I thank you very much.
Campbell: Sure.

Caudill: We wish you the best.
Campbell: Well, that's for what they did for my Uncle Clifton sixty years ago, seventy years ago, I guess almost.

Living Out the Drama:
An Interview with Will Campbell

Kenneth L. Gibble / 1984

From the *Christian Century*, May 30, 1984, 570–74. Reprinted with permission of the author.

Irascible and often irreverent, Will Campbell has spent his sixty years elevating iconoclasm to a vocation. His darts have been aimed at such diverse targets as American civil religion, the electronic church, the institutional church, theological education, racism, and liberalism.

In the unlikely event that Will Campbell would choose to list his credentials, they would reveal that he was educated at Tulane, Wake Forest, and Yale, where he received his BD in 1952. He served as a consultant on race relations for the National Council of Churches in the 1950s and '60s. As a member of the Committee of Southern Churchmen, he wrote and coedited books with J. Y. Holloway, but he first gained national recognition as a writer with the award-winning and self-revealing *Brother to a Dragonfly* (Seabury, 1977). Since then he has written two novels, *The Glad River* (Holt, Rinehart & Winston, 1982) and *Cecilia's Sin* (Mercer University Press, 1983).

In private conversation, Campbell prefers to talk about his "real work"— that of being a minister-at-large to the imprisoned, the troubled, the dying— or of his time spent on the road as a cook for his friend country singer Waylon Jennings, or of his friendship with cartoonists Jules Pfeiffer and Doug Marlette. (Campbell denies that Marlette's character, the Rev. Will B. Dunn, is modeled on himself: "Sure the Rev. Will B. Dunn whittles just like I do. But he whittles with a big barrow knife and I use a little penknife. And the dead giveaway is that while I chew Beechnut tobacco, the Rev. Dunn chews Red Man.")

My interview with Will Campbell took place outside the log cabin where he does most of his writing at his home in Mount Juliet, Tennessee. "I swapped a mule to get the logs for this cabin," he said as we walked past some ungainly fowl milling in the backyard. "Those? They're guinea hens. One of my visitors told me that the difference between Flannery O'Connor and Will Campbell is summed up by the fact that she raised peacocks and I raise guinea hens." The self-depreciating laughter that accompanied this anecdote was to punctuate our conversation at frequent intervals.

Kenneth Gibble: In *Brother to a Dragonfly*, you wrote that you had once told your brother Joe, "All I ever wanted was to be a preacher." Does that still hold? And is that your vocation?

Will Campbell: Sure it still holds. But I get nervous about that word "vocation." My vocation—if you mean "calling"—is no different from that of any other baptized believer. My vocation is living out the drama. One of the characters in *The Glad River* says, "The trouble began when someone dreamed up the public-relations gimmick, 'full-time Christian service.'" We started confusing baptism with ordination and *paying* one another to be Christian, to be part of the drama. I don't buy that. There's very little in the New Testament I can find about ordination. There's quite a bit about baptism.

Gibble: Does some institutional body recognize your ordination, or is that not even relevant for you?

Campbell: It's not relevant for *me*. But hanging on my wall is a plain piece of paper full of misspelled words and typos that the Baptist preacher who ordained me typed up on that occasion. It's signed by my daddy and uncle and cousin and the country preacher. And nobody can take that away from me.

There was an effort made to do so some years back, even though I didn't know about it at the time. With the Baptists, the local church does the ordaining. I think that's a good idea, but sometimes it can come back to haunt you. Sometimes a church begins to wonder, "What if we made a mistake?" Or, in my case, "What if we ordained some radical, a nigger lover?" So the folks back in that country church decided that if they had *given* the ordination, they could also take it away. The only thing that stopped them, apparently, was that a couple of guys I'd grown up with said, "If you try to take Will's ordination away, we'll filibuster. We'll stand on the church floor till doomsday speaking against it." The Baptists are no different from anybody else; their idol is "harmony within the fellowship." So they just let the issue drop.

But even if it had gone through, that document would continue to hang on my kitchen wall, glued on top of my college and seminary degrees and other alleged honors. That piece of paper is my marching orders.

Gibble: Would you call yourself an anti-intellectual?

Campbell: Yes. But you've got to be an intellectual before you can be an anti-intellectual. My quarrel with the academy is with its arrogance. Learning is not an ultimate. Our three children all have at least one degree from an institution of so-called higher education. I'm glad of that, glad they know the difference between the humor of Polonius and Minnie Pearl, or between Beaujolais and Ripple. But that has nothing whatsoever to do with the Christian faith.

I'm not a scholar, don't try to be one and don't *want* to be, but when I need a scholar I find one. Every so often, I'll go down to Vanderbilt and blast the hell out of them in some context or other. Then the next day, I'll call up one of the faculty and say, "Tell me about so and so." And he or she will say, "Sure, I'll tell you, Will, but I'm surprised you're calling me. I work at Vanderbilt Divinity School." And I'll say, "I know where you work. I have nothing against scholarship." It's just that I'm not going to worship it or say it's exempt from hubris.

Gibble: You've also spoken out against civil religion. What are the church-state issues these days?

Campbell: They're all over the place. Take this school-prayer thing. One night the country picker Tom T. Hall and I were arguing about it. He was saying, "What's wrong with prayer in schools? That's no big deal," and of course I was saying it *is* a big deal; who's going to write the prayers and so on. So finally Tom T. says, "Look, it's very simple. You make it homework. If the teacher can assign my boy an hour of calculus and a half hour of typing practice, she can certainly say, "Now before you come back in the morning, you spend five minutes in prayer and meditation. Your parents can help you." And you know, he might be on to something!

Gibble: In *Glad River* and *Cecilia's Sin*, you almost seem to be saying that no "Baptist," which is your word for committed Christian, can participate in Caesar's kingdom in any way—serve on a jury, pay taxes, register for the draft. But most Christians, even people like the Amish, can't live that way. Where do you draw the line at what you will or won't do in regard to the state's demands?

Campbell: I don't try to draw those lines. I think that when Jesus said, "Give Caesar what belongs to Caesar," he was drawing on his tremendous sense of humor. He held up this worthless coin and said, "Okay, then, give him a quarter." In other words, give him *nothing*.

But we come along and say, "Jesus told us to render unto Caesar what is Caesar's, so we know *something* belongs to Caesar. Now what is it?" And we end up giving Caesar everything. We give him power to execute people who break his laws. We give him power to say to pregnant women, "You can kill these babies if you want to," and so on.

I pay taxes, but I don't celebrate it. I repent of it. So on the Fourth of July I ring the bells around this place, not in celebration, but in lamentation for the shameful history of this country in which I live and prosper. And I might add that the history of any other country is not much different. But once you start saying, "God made this country great," then you can justify anything under the sun, including blowing people's sweetbreads right through their earholes.

Gibble: What political figures do you admire today?
Campbell: None.

Gibble: That didn't take long! What do you make of the Jimmy Carter phenomenon?
Campbell: It was a Babel tower. We can't do any better by putting one of our own Caesars in charge. Caesar is Caesar. The military buildup we've got today didn't start under Ronald Reagan. If someone who is president would say, "I'm representing another kingdom and in that kingdom we don't go to war," he'd be impeached. And he *should* be impeached, because he's sworn to uphold the Constitution of a sovereign nation, and that Constitution says we're going to defend this piece of geography by whatever means it takes.

Our call is not to be Caesar; our call is to be in conflict with Caesar. And we *will* be in conflict, because of the nature of the two critters. Now, I do a lot of talking about the evils of institutions. But I do participate in institutions all the time. So I try not to say, "I'm bowing down and putting this pinch of incense on Caesar's altar as my reasonable service because that is what the Lord expects of me." My old friend Elbert Jean says when we're bringing that incense, we need to lean over and snicker a little bit and say, "I know who's back there; I know who's doing it to me." Then we can hang on to some degree of our humanity. Otherwise we're equating this act of unfaithfulness with faith. That is the unpardonable sin; that is apostasy.

Gibble: And liberals and conservatives alike commit this sin.
Campbell: Sure. I've been hard on the electronic church. I go places where they like to hear me on that subject. Especially up North. Not long ago I was

up in Wisconsin, and I could tell what they wanted to hear about was the decadent South. So I said to myself, okay, I'll give them some of that. I told them about a friend of mine, an investigative journalist who began looking into the financial dealings of the PTL Club. He found a bunch of interesting things, one of which was that Jim and Tammy Bakker live in this Florida condominium that's got mirrors on the walls from floor to ceiling so you can see the ocean any way you turn. And I assume you can see yourself, too.

Then I said, "All that stuff was built off the backs of the poor. If you chase wealth back far enough, you get into the mines and the fields. It's not the boss man who's digging the coal out of the ground and raising the crops. What's wrong with all this affluence in the name of the gentle Jesus is that it's built off the exploitation of the poor." And, of course, everybody listening was in general agreement.

So I paused and said, "All right, what's the difference between that and the pope's jewels, or all those Lutheran and Presbyterian and Methodist steeples out there casting shadows on whores and pimps and addicts and bums with—let's be honest—seldom a gesture in their direction from any of us proportionate to what we spend on ourselves? If you push it to its conclusion, the difference is simply one of taste."

So someone got up and said, "Surely you're not saying that the Sistine Chapel is as ugly as some goddamn condominium with mirrors on the walls?" I answered by saying that I guess it's all right for the poor peasants of Italy to put their pennies in the box for the Sistine Chapel, but it's not all right for the widow on Social Security or the pulpwood haulers of Georgia and Alabama to send their $5 and $10 to the TV preachers. Then what we're talking about is the annihilation of the hillbillies and rednecks. And I think when you get right down to it, that's what the liberals' upset over the electronic church and Jerry Falwell and the Moral Majority is all about.

Gibble: Let's talk about Will Campbell the writer.
Campbell: I'm not a professional writer. I don't think of myself as a writer. It seems too presumptuous. But I've always liked to write. When I was a kid going to a little country school, the teacher would assign us themes on different subjects. I'd write cowboy stories instead. I'd stay up until Mama made me go to bed. If I got called on first in class the next day—and the other kids all hoped I would—it would take me the whole period just to read my story.

But I'm not disciplined enough to be a real writer. The professional writers I know tell me they write six or seven days a week. When my friend Walker Percy found out I was working on a novel, he said, "I'm not sure you can do that, Will. You're a good writer, but the only way to write a novel is to wander up to the brink of total insanity and then go in and finish it. Then see what you can salvage of your senses when you're through. You are capable of getting up to the brink, but then somebody will stub a toe and you'll go running off to play priest."

I thought he was probably right, but I figured I'd try it anyway.

Gibble: Do you preach in your novels?
Campbell: Do you remember the movie *Never on Sunday*?

Gibble: The one about the prostitute?
Campbell: Right. When people ask me what I do, I say I'm a Baptist preacher, but never on Sunday. Some of them get the symbolism of that and others don't.

Gibble: Some critics would claim you can't be a novelist and a preacher, too—that if you try to do both what you produce isn't art, isn't literature. Does such criticism bother you?
Campbell: It doesn't bother me in the least.

Gibble: You don't care what the critics say?
Campbell: Well, that's not quite true. We all "care" what other people say. The worst review *Glad River* got came from Jonathan Yardley, what had reviewed *Dragonfly* most effusively. But in his *Glad River* review, he largely reviewed *me*, not the book. I thought that was unfair. *I* got a favorable review, but his last sentence was: "his is a noble man and he has done noble deeds, but he's not a novelist."

Not true. That's like saying a peg-legged man is not a runner. You can say he lost the race or he shouldn't have chosen to be a runner. But if he gets out there on the course, even if he falls down and the splinters that peg leg and has to be dragged off the track, you can't say he's not a runner. Just say he's a poor runner.

So, yes, I care, but I'm not going to change direction because I know what the Bernard Baruchs of the literary world are looking for. Besides, I don't buy this idea that a preacher who writes novels is not a novelist. Was there no preaching in *Moby Dick*, or in Shakespeare's plays? Everybody is a propagandist, otherwise there's no use in talking to one another. I don't care if a person is writing or teaching auto mechanics, that person ought to be engaged in teaching values.

When I was in school, even philosophy professors would say, "It's not my job to teach values." Well, then, what *is* their job? That's one of my criticisms of theological education. I think most kids today want to know what horse you're betting on, what you're staking your life on. But educators are cagey because they're not betting on a damn thing, except maybe "scholarship," and that's a pretty shaky reed.

Gibble: Do you have a particular audience you write for?

Campbell: I've never thought about that. I guess it's the same people who sit in church pews. They're the ones claiming some allegiance to Christ, and I think I'm calling us all to task on how far we're missing the mark. Part of what I'm about, I suppose, is trying to convert those who don't have this allegiance, though I don't do that consciously. Usually when people talk about evangelism, what they really mean is recruitment.

Jessi Colter, Waylon Jennings's wife, is a very religious woman, a Pentecostal. She worries a lot about Waylon's soul. One night we were riding down in the interstate around two in the morning and I asked him, "Waylon, what do you believe?" And he said, "Yeah!"

I got to thinking about that, and you know, it just might be the most profound affirmation of faith I've ever heard. "I believe, help my unbelief, period." What is there to say after that?

Gibble: What's the hardest part of writing for you?

Campbell: Getting the time to do it, an uninterrupted stretch without somebody coming and saying, as one person did this summer, "I've got incurable, inoperable cancer. They tell me I've got two to eight months to live. I'm an atheist, I don't believe a goddamn thing, and I want you to help me die." So like an idiot I said, "Do you want to talk about the God who damns everything you don't believe?" And she said, "Don't counsel me, please." And she was right.

Or somebody lands in jail or I've got to go make a speech somewhere. I don't usually say, "I've got more important things to do," because writing is not the most important thing I do. It's almost my hobby.

Gibble: Which of your books would you like to be remembered for?

Campbell: Certainly the most meaningful book so far was *Brother to a Dragonfly* because the subject was so nearly sacred. It was at once very painful and very rewarding. I will never be sorry I wrote it, though it did bring a great deal of pain. My brother's first wife sued me for three quarters of a million dollars. That was very painful and depressing, almost in the clinical sense. I couldn't deal with it. I couldn't figure out why she did it.

It's not that I had visions of the Mayflower van pulling up and by being dispossessed. I know that if there is anything libelous or slanderous or vicious in that book, then all of us might as well melt our typewriters.

Part of it, I guess, was like having a beautiful little child and everybody saying what a lovely, curly-headed cherub you've got—there wasn't one bad review of *Dragonfly*—and then somebody coming along and dumping a bucket of slop over that child's head.

I think *The Glad River* is a better book in terms of creative writing. I got some bad reviews on it, but some good ones too. Some of the negative comments came because critics don't like genre hoppers. They wanted a continuation of *Dragonfly*. Critics like to get writers pegged in particular holes and if they pop their heads up in different ones, like Bugs Bunny, then WHOOMP: "Get back over there in *your* hole."

Gibble: Did you feel exposed, naked, after writing such an intensely personal book as *Dragonfly*?
Campbell: Yes. But I discovered long ago that the only way we learn from one another is by being willing to bare as much about ourselves as our nervous systems will let us, which is never very much. Most of us are too busy girding our loins and saying, "There are no warts on my rear end; I'm smooth and clean and good." Consequentially, we don't learn from each other. It did concern me that in *Dragonfly* I was exposing people other than myself. But I had strong support from my immediate family—my father, my sister, my younger brother, although *he* had some problems with the language. So did some other people! Christian bookstores wouldn't carry it, it had too many "ugly" words for them. But I'd learned long ago what the really ugly words are.

I *was* concerned about my father's reaction to the language. I'd never heard him say anything stronger than "heck" or "durn." But one day he told someone in my presence (and I knew he was really addressing me), "Truth is, most of us were taught one way of talking in the living room, but you get in the back of the pasture and the mule won't go or the mowing machine breaks down, you probably talk another way. My boy just told it the way it was."

Gibble: Both *The Glad River* and *Cecilia's Sin* were personal too, but in a different way.

Campbell: Sure, fiction can be just as autobiographical as nonfiction. Walker Percy took me to talk for that on *Glad River*. When he read the manuscript, he didn't like it.

"Your main character, Doops, is you, Will," he said.

"I guess so," I said. "Isn't Will Barrett [in Percy's novel *The Second Coming*] *you?*"

He said, "Yeah, probably."

But he kept trimming around the edges with his comments. "There aren't any women in this story. Are these three guys gay or what?"

I said, "They're just close friends—brothers, if you like. What else is wrong with the book?"

"Well, you got this guy Doops out there in the jungle for three days and nights and nothing happens. You've got to have Doops *do* something. Try to pull the Jap out of his mudhole or give him an aspirin or wipe his ass or something. There's a rule in fiction writing: 'Thou shalt not go for three days and three nights without doing *something*.'"

I said, "Don't give me that crap, Walker. Will Barrett falls down on the golf course, and it takes fifty-seven pages to get him off that course."

So he says, "Okay, the real problem I have with this book is the theological problem. You've committed the greatest Christian heresy, the romantic heresy. The baptism in the book is not a Christian baptism, it's a romantic baptism. The burial is not a Christian burial, it's a romantic burial."

So I change one paragraph of the book, and when it was published, he called me late one night and said, "Will, I just wanted to tell you this book is one hell of a novel. Goodbye."

Gibble: Was your change a way to get rid of the Donatist heresy?

Campbell: Yeah. Walker Percy had quoted Latin passages about the efficacy of the sacrament not depending on the morality of the priest and all that, so in the scene where Doops is refusing to be baptized, I had Kingston say to him, "Why don't you just go ahead and let the guy baptize you? It don't matter whether he's a son of a bitch or not. A priest don't have anything to do with it." And that's all it needed. It was my way of saying, "You see, Walker, I know better!"

Interview with
Reverend Will Campbell

Orlando Bagwell / 1985

From *Eyes on the Prize: America's Civil Rights Years, 1954–1965*, a documentary in six episodes produced by Blackside, Inc., and originally released from January 21 to February 25, 1987. Transcription from Henry Hampton Collection, Washington University Libraries Department of Special Collections. Interview conducted November 3, 1985. Reprinted with permission.

Interviewer: Reverend Campbell, I'd like to talk first about the South and in particular Nashville and the two churches: the black church and the white church, and where they were at, say, in 1960, between the fifties and sixties. Just give me an identity for the South at that time.

Rev. Will D. Campbell: Well, of course, the churches were like the rest of society, rigidly segregated so that you had a First Baptist Church, which was white, on Broadway. Then you had a First Baptist Church, which is now called the First Baptist Capitol Hill, which was black—a hundred years earlier, they had been one. And one of the great tragedies, I think, for the institutional church was that they did split following the Civil War, they were one church then. And the pastor of the First Baptist Church in 1960, Reverend Kelly Miller Smith, First Baptist Church of Capitol Hill, which was the black church, just a few blocks from the white First Baptist Church—both of them were in a massive building campaign, so the Pastor Reverend Smith wrote to the Pastor of the white church and said, Look, it hasn't been that long ago by God's time, a hundred years, that we were one church. Now we find ourselves a few blocks apart, we're both in a massive building campaign. Why don't we at least talk in terms of building one church? And the response was our people feel there are too few good churches in downtown Nashville, not too many—very evasive things. So the structured church was—there was this breach that black people didn't go to church with white people and vice versa.

Interviewer: Now in 1960, when the sit-ins begin and the protest campaign in Nashville begins, how does that play into the minds of people in terms of how they're doing with each other and just the idea of, you know, the Christian church and people not being able to really come to grips with one another? How [are] the churches playing into that, with Vanderbilt as a major institution at that time?

Campbell: Yeah, well, of course, the white established structured church tried very hard not to deal with it at all, just simply ignore it.

Interviewer: You have to give me what all those things are.

Campbell: Okay, let's go back then again and I'm not sure of what you're asking me to talk about here. Now are you going to ask a question or do you just want me to start talking?

Interviewer: I'll ask a question. Talking about Vanderbilt and bring in Jim Lawson and him being expelled and the role Vanderbilt was playing as a part of that effect on . . .

Campbell: Yeah, okay. James Lawson was a student at Vanderbilt Divinity School—was, I believe, the first black student. He was more active perhaps in the training and preparing the young people in Nashville for the sit-in movement because he had been in prison himself during the Korean War. He was a C.O. [conscientious objector] resister, had refused to register for the draft and had been sent to federal prison because of that. Vanderbilt took the position when the sit-ins began—and he was charged by the city with criminal anarchy—that they were not expelling him because of his involvement in the freedom movement, or the sit-in movement, but because he was—had violated a state statute. Now keep in mind that he had not been convicted of this when he was expelled. He was simply charged with this, arrested and thrown in prison, but he was expelled. The black church was virtually unanimously for him. The white churches, those who even would bother to discuss it among themselves, were almost unanimously against it. Now that is not to say that there were not individuals within the white church both at Vanderbilt University and in the structured church, the steeples as I call them, there were individuals, but you always have to distinguish between individuals and institutions. Vanderbilt, as an institution, was in my judgment totally irresponsible, almost criminal in their actions toward James Lawson. Individuals within that faculty and within the Vanderbilt community at large, many individuals, were outspoken on behalf of James Lawson, were very much in sympathy with him. But institutions are so powerful and, in my judgment, so evil, that it made no difference, you know, these faculty people could say—and the medical student faculty, almost all of them, threatened to resign. The divinity faculty did on one occasion, almost all of them resigned. But the institution goes pell-mell on its way and says what . . . you know, this guy is a threat to the institution. And if something becomes a threat to the institution, then that institution is just going to push it out of its way, which is precisely what happened. He was expelled and the institution survived and went on.

Interviewer: Now in 1960 people say that Nashville was a pretty progressive city, especially in terms of race, that they had city employees who were black. There were moves, people were saying there were moves—movement in the city to deal with the race issue, and that this was not then—the protest movement was just too—wasn't time, it was like pushing them too fast. Can you talk about that, and the feelings of the community towards, about that whole . . .

Campbell: I think in 1960, Nashville was a progressive city, but so was Little Rock, Arkansas, in 1957 when Governor Faubus called out the troops to stop this horrendous onslaught of nine black children coming to Central High School. So was New Orleans, where you had serious riots the same year and the following year, and it took marshals to escort one child through the lines and so on. But . . . when you say progressive, I think it reflected a mood within a large group of individuals, but when those individuals go up against structures and institutions and—well, let's take segregation as an institutionalized reality in Nashville—then those individuals made little or no difference. So, if you came and talked to X number of white and black in Nashville in 1960, or the late fifties, you might well go away saying, well, this city can do anything it wants to because it has an enlightened citizenry. But these evil structures are so institutionalized and so demonic and so difficult to deal with that these quote "enlightened" individuals were relatively powerless.

Interviewer: Okay now, going, getting into the movement and say, Looby's house is bombed. What happened to the city at that point? How did people respond?

Campbell: Mr. Z. Alexander Looby, who was a great man, a black attorney, conservative politically, a Lincoln Republican of many years, no one could accuse him of being a wild-eyed radical politically. And when his house was bombed or dynamited, I think it solidified especially the black community, and it enraged a segment of the white community in a fashion that nothing else had. When you had the hundred or hundreds of black students coming down and sitting in at the Woolworth stores and so on, all of the five and dime stores, and department stores, that was one thing, because students are supposed to be irresponsible, you know, and wild eyed, and so you just kind of shrug that off. And if the police get a little rough, you know, and overzealous and throwing—and pack thirty into a paddy wagon that's designed for eight—well, after all, you know, they're just students. But this elderly man who had been a citizen, a lawyer, a councilman, and so on, over the years, and when his house is in a rubble, this did outrage a lot of people. Now, I would have to acknowledge, much as I would like to say, being afflicted with this incurable skin disease called lightness, that it solidified the white community to go out and join the marches—it did not. But there was the mass march to City Hall, and there was a white mayor who came out there and who with considerable prodding from that brilliant and beautiful leader named Diane Nash, who kept pushing him—but, Mr. Mayor, you are our mayor, sir, do you think that segregation is morally defendable? And he eventually had to say, I do not. Now that, in my judgment, was the turning point. That encounter was a turning point. So you had a white mayor of a leading city reflecting on this alleged progressive characteristic of the city. And once he says this, and then you have a leading black citizen with his house dynamited, now it goes back to the dynamiting, so that whoever set off that dynamite or bomb blast, did more to integrate the lunch counters and the department stores in Nashville, I think, than all the sit-ins combined.

Interviewer: Tell me about that letter with Jim Lawson and his attempts to—he was going to resign rather than letting them expel him.
Campbell: Well, the pressures had been mounting, of course, for days, and Jim Lawson, being a considerate and a gentle person basically, agreed to withdraw voluntarily from Vanderbilt University, from the divinity school, called me and asked me to come over to go over the letter he had prepared the night before—he and his wife, who had been my secretary, Dorothy Wood—and my position was, no, you don't do that. You don't let them off the hook, that you're going to go, you're going to have to leave, Jim, but make them kick you out so that they and the world will know what this— where this institution stands and what it's up to, which is what he did then. When he went over to the meeting that had been convened for the purpose

of announcing that Mr. Lawson had agreed to withdraw and for the sake of harmony and peace in the Vanderbilt fellowship here. And when Jim said, I'm not withdrawing, of course, there was a great deal of hostility and the dean of [unintelligible] asked all outsiders to leave and so the press people started leaving and then he looked at me and said, this is a family matter. And, so I, being a gentleman too, started to leave, and Jim and some of the other white students caught my jacket and said to the dean, he is family, which I considered that I was family. I had been very much involved in the entire situation because of the relationship of his wife being my secretary and working with me, and he being a friend also. But had he resigned on his own, I think it would have been a totally different picture that the world would have got of what was going on in Nashville, because they would have shrugged it off and said, now everybody's happy, there's no—but in reality this—there might have been a little smooth scar healed over, but underneath it was still seething cauldron of infection which had to erupt, had to erupt sometime, and it might as well have been then, and there.

Interviewer: That episode on the steps of the statehouse and not being an end or beginning, talk to me about that.

Campbell: Yes, when Diane Nash, later Diane Bevel, had the confrontation with Mayor West, and for the first time, the mayor of this city went on record as saying that merchants cannot morally justify taking people's money, but giving them unequal service in terms of hiring, of restroom facilities, of eating facilities, drinking fountains, and so on. This was the first crack in the frozen pond of racial segregation in this city. It did not mean the melting of the ice when everything was over, but it was a starting point, and so here the mayor has said this. Now, before anything really was accomplished, there had to be the Easter boycott of the stores, the virtual drying up of the downtown area and I think for the first time the merchants and the city officials realized that we were talking more than just the right to a hamburger and a cup of coffee at the five-and-ten-cent store. That we are talking about employment, we're talking about fairness in general, and treating people as human beings, and really what we're talking about, and this was the most frightening of all, that we were talking about a redistribution of America's wealth. Just as when the quote—make a big jump here from Nashville to the national church scene—when James Forman walked into Riverside Church in New York and read the manifesto, talking about reparation for misdeeds of white churches, and demanding of white churches that they give $50 million or whatever, of their vast wealth—for the first time the national scene saw that what we're talking about is more than a cup of coffee and a hamburger. I think you, I gave you more than you asked for, but—

Interviewer: Okay, what were your feelings about them turning back at that point, and bring John Seigenthaler's name into your . . .

Campbell: Well, certainly it was mixed. John Seigenthaler, who had been the editor of the local newspaper and a journalist with the Nashville *Tennessean*—was at that time working with Attorney General Kennedy, as I recall, and asked me if I had enough influence to get the movement to turn back when Bull Connor in Birmingham had, of course, brought the Freedom Riders back to the county line and so on. And it was obvious that the Nashville kids, as we called them, were going to continue this, and my feelings were mixed. Number one, having been born and reared in this city and knowing the climate in the white community there, I really believed they would be killed. And so I didn't want people like John Lewis and Diane Nash dying at the hands of quote "my people" in Mississippi. On the other hand, I knew that in terms of the long-range goals of the movement, and the fierce determination and dedication of those youngsters at the time, you know, they were like eighteen, nineteen years old. I knew they were going to do it, and there was nothing I could do but weep for what I was certain was going to happen, and for the tragedy even if it didn't happen, that the notion that a group of people can't ride through my state in a Greyhound bus is rather overwhelming.

Interviewer: You used that term in your book of Lunesean reality when you're talking about the Willie McGee execution. I'd like you to view in that same frame of mind, talk about Montgomery when you came in to see John Seigenthaler in the hospital, what you encountered there.

Campbell: Was that Mother's Day?

Interviewer: No, this was after, this was . . . around the 26 of May, this was after the Montgomery ambush.

Campbell: I remember that. When the Freedom Riders reached Montgomery, and apparently the arrangement had been made that there would be no police protection for X number of minutes, five minutes or whatever, so that a mob was set loose to do what they will. And John Seigenthaler was there as a personal representative of the president, and two young women were trying to get into a cab and were being turned away and were being roughed up and John went over and said, "I am a personal representative of the president." And that's the last thing he remembered saying for a long time because someone caught him over the back of the head with a steel pipe and he lay in the sun there for a long time. And I was not present, I was not there at the time, and a friend of mine—a young attorney here—George Baird and I, chartered a little plane the next morning, Sunday morning. And John, we thought he was in critical condition, of course they didn't know how seriously he was hurt, but he was in the hospital there. He used to kid me when I was working for the National Council of Churches, he'd say, "Oh, here comes the guy who represents forty million Protestants," and of course we didn't represent anybody, you know. So I walked into the room and I said in his hospital room, and the priest was on his way out, and I thought oh lord, is he gone and they're doing unction on John Seigenthaler? And I said, "John, I'm here representing forty million Protestants," and he threw me the bottle of holy water and he said, "Well here, I think one of your forty million damned near killed me yesterday down at that bus station." And I knew John was going to be okay.

Interviewer: Talk to me about driving through the city and listening in on sermons.
Campbell: And driving around after—

Interviewer: Start again please.
Campbell: Where do you want me to start?

Interviewer: Why don't you start about, driving through, and listening to sermons and what you would hear and what it meant to you.
Campbell: Well, after the visit with John, I wanted to go and see the students in various hospitals. There was a black St. Jude's, I believe was the name of the Catholic-operated hospital on the edge of town where the Freedom Riders had been taken, black and white. And some of them were in critical condition and I went to visit them and, of course I was lost and scared and just driving, at times, aimlessly around the city, at eleven o'clock on Sunday morning . . . and here was a city that had been, the day before, in utter chaos. And people were being clubbed and beaten and the city was in turmoil, and not one preacher, and I kept moving the knob and listening to this sermon and that one, over the hour or so time there, and you might as well have been on a different planet, you know, that there was no mention of this in sermons, no prayer for forgiveness, to say nothing of deliverance.

And so that this—this sharp cleavage between what was happening in the black churches of Montgomery where mass meetings were going on every night, and I am certain that if a black preacher had been on the radio that day there would have been mention of this, both in prayer, in praise, in homily, and in psalm. But the white church—there was no mention of this, because it is controversial, and there's one thing sacred in any institution and that's harmony.

Interviewer: Okay, if you could explain to Orlando first of all, how you first heard about the murder of Emmett Till and what your own personal reaction was, what that meant to you.

Campbell: Well, I heard about it in the newspapers . . . I read of the murder of a young black child really, fifteen years old, named Emmett Till, in the newspapers and of course on the radio. And I was director of religious life at the time at the University of Mississippi, and I knew that this man would never, whoever had committed this, would never be convicted. And there was a long drawn-out trial, and in all fairness to the judge in the case—I watched some of it in the courtroom—I think he did the best he could, but the two men who were charged with this murder were at the time heroes. Now the strange part of it is, as soon as the trial was over, and Mr. William Bradley Hewitt [sic, author of the article was William Bradford Huie] wrote a story for a magazine showing the check that he had made out to them to tell the real story, where they said, yeah, we took him down there and you know, we beat him and then killed him and threw him in the river, Tallahatchie River, and so on. Those people were nobodies after that. They were disgraced, which is a strange conflict and dichotomy in southern society that while they were being accused of this crime, we have to rally to their defense and take up money, and hire lawyers, and all the rest. But then when it's over, look, why did you have to disgrace us like that, now get out of town, we don't really want to see you again.

Interviewer: Do you have a sense of what the reaction, if any, from white Mississippians in general was to the news of that, first of the lynching and then of the trial and the verdict?

Campbell: It's very difficult to believe that in 1955 intelligent, civilized, and often sophisticated people would say, well, that didn't really happen, that the NAACP, which was considered the radicals at the time, had this boy killed and thrown in the river to embarrass white Mississippi, or to raise money and so on. All kinds of stories, or that wasn't really his body, his mother discredited, that they—some black undertaker from Chicago—brought a bum down here who had died of a drug overdose on the streets and threw it in the river and Emmett Till's back in Chicago laughing at us. And these things, which is today impossible—even though I lived through it and experienced it—to believe that those things were being seriously said and reported in allegedly responsible organs of the media . . . but it happened.

Interviewer: Good.
Campbell: All right.

The Futility of Fighting
Over What We Believe

Bill McNabb / 1990

From the *Wittenburg Door Magazine*, March/April 1990. Reprinted with the permission of Anthony Ole, publisher, *The Door*.

Will Campbell is weird—a good kind of weird, but weird, nonetheless. He's ornery. Will usually says what he thinks . . . when he thinks it. He has been known to sip a Jack Daniels or two, and his language is . . . well . . . spicy.

Will is a Baptist preacher, an author, and a farmer. But mainly, Will Campbell is a writer—a darned good one. His books *Glad River*, *Brother to a Dragonfly*, and *Forty Acres and a Goat* are probably three of the best books you'll ever read.

Will's a talker, too. A storyteller. Mostly though, he's a truthteller. Will kinda tricks ya. You think you're talking to some ignorant cornpone from Tennessee, and who you're really talkin' to is a Yale-educated preacher whose insights into the Gospel have liberated him from the structures that so often intimidate the rest of us.

Not only is Will Campbell not intimidated by institutions, he wasn't even intimidated by *us*—even though we sent *The Door*'s crack interviewer, Bill McNabb, to interview him. That would intimidate most anyone . . . but not Will Campbell. He just took a look at Bill and said, "Well, where's the Jack Daniels?" After Bill spent an hour locating it, Will consented to the interview. What follows are the comments made between sips of J.D. late into the night somewhere in Los Angeles.

Bill McNabb: Let's talk about the Church.
Will Campbell: What is it?

Bill McNabb: *We* ask the questions. What is the Church?
Will Campbell: I have no idea.

Bill McNabb: It was *your* question.
Will Campbell: I know. That's why I was asking you. Hell, I don't know what the Church is. Jesus said something about the fact that He was going to *build* the Church. He did say that nothing would prevail over it . . . even the gates of Hell, but He didn't ask me to build it. And He certainly didn't ask me to define it. I *believe* the Church *is* at work in the world only because of my faith in this Jesus person. Trouble is, I don't know what Jesus is up to or where His Church is. That's good.

Bill McNabb: Why is that?
Will Campbell: Because if I found the Church, then I'd give it a name and start runnin' it.

Bill McNabb: What's wrong with that? Then we'd call you a minister, which is what you are.
Will Campbell: Only problem is, runnin' a church is not ministry, it's runnin' an office, visitin' the sick, preparin' sermons, and workin' with the sacramental chores. That's just administration. Nothin' wrong with it, you know, but it ain't ministry. I think the word ministry is rather presumptuous anyway. Sounds kind imperialistic to me—you know, I can do something for you better than you can do yourself.

Bill McNabb: But you *are* a minister.
Will Campbell: Well, I think I'm more like a preacher without a steeple. Kinda like a bootleg preacher.

Bill McNabb: Bootleg preacher? What does that mean?
Will Campbell: It means I don't "minister" for the institutional church—the steeple. *No* institution can be trusted, including the steeple. They are all after our souls—*all* of them. It means that I refuse to let any institution or ideology tell me how to do my ministry. There are no conditions, *ever*, in the New Testament. No ideology in the New Testament, either. II Corinthians 5 makes it very clear that when one is in Christ he/she is a new creature. No longer do we consider anyone by human standards or human categories. That is an exceedingly radical bit of news. When one is in Christ, human

categories are no longer applicable. But an institution is a human category and every institution is self-loving, self-regarding, and self-protecting, and anything bad for the institution it proclaims as unchristian.

Bill McNabb: Hm-mm-mm. Of course, we don't know many bootleg ministers. In fact, you're the only one we know. What would you say to ministers who work within the institution?

Will Campbell: I would say "Don't trust it." *Don't trust it.* That doesn't mean that God doesn't work wherever God chooses, so I wouldn't rule out the stained glass and the mahogany pews and the silver chalices. I don't rule *any* of that out. I am just trying to say that if God is the God of the universe, don't try to put God in this pigeonhole and say, "If you want to be with God, come to this edifice or this steeple or serve this particular cause."

Bill McNabb: But Will, we *do* have steeples, we *do* have institutions and almost all of us are part of them. What are you suggesting? Burn them down?

Will Campbell: I know that if we could abolish all institutions today, tomorrow we'd start rebuilding them. Institutions are inevitable, I know that. *I* work within them all the time, I don't claim not to. But I try and say, "I'm working *within* this particular institution . . . *but I don't trust you.* I bend over to put the pinch of incense on the pagan altars all the time, but I try to remember to snicker a little bit when I do. I'm bending over, yes, but if I can snicker, then I maintain a little of my humanity, which what to be "in Christ" means, near as I can tell.

Bill McNabb: If you don't trust the institutional church, are you saying it is *bad???*

Will Campbell: I am saying that in my judgment the institutional church is standing today where the rich young ruler stood—both are rich, powerful, and good. I never say the church is bad. Obviously, it's not a bad outfit: the institutional church—structure—is a good outfit. It is also very powerful. It is also very, very rich. So rich that if the structure did what the rich young ruler was told to do, then we could lick the problem of poverty in this country overnight. Let's suppose the structured church *did* sell all of their buildings, parking lots, computers, Betty Crocker kitchens, skating rinks, and gymnasium. What would happen?

Bill McNabb: You raised the issue first. You answer the question.

Will Campbell: Well, I have some hunches about what might happen. We might sing the Psalms for the first time in our lives. An unemployed preacher might come by wanting something to eat, and we might experience the supper of our Lord for the first time in our lives.

Bill McNabb: We've been talking about institutional structures. Let's talk specifically about institutional religion.

Will Campbell: The evil of institutional religion is the result of two confusions. The first confusion is to confuse belief with faith. Belief is not faith. The devils believe. The inquisitions, the holy wars, and the modern-day internal warfare within denominations like the Southern Baptists are never about faith. They're always about belief. Belief is always passive. That's why we kill people—because of what they believe, not because of what they do. But faith is *active*. Faith implies doubt. Paul had doubts at the end of his life—"What if I, after having preached the way to others, have missed the way myself?" Today we are bombarded with the theology of certitude which says, "I've found it. I've got it. If you don't *believe* the way *I* believe, then you are out." That kind of theology has nothing to do with faith. Actually, we confuse the things we wish for with the things we hope in. We confuse wish and hope.

Bill McNabb: You lost us again. What do you mean?

Will Campbell: I wish for a world without nuclear bombs. I wish for a world where everyone would have a home, a place to sleep at night. I wish for a world where children are not abused. I wish for a world that is drug free. But none of those wishes are what my hope is in. I may or may not see my wishes come true, but my hope is in eternal things. God will have the last word. I have to admit, if I had been God, I would not have made us quite as free as He created us. I wouldn't have made us puppets, but I would have created a little string so if some cat—

Bill McNabb: Cat?

Will Campbell: I'm old. Okay? So if some cat was on the verge of blowing up the universe I could jerk the string and say, "Nope, you're not going to do that." But no, we're just as free as God. We can blow this universe up. *Even so, that is not the last word.* But you know what troubles me?

Bill McNabb: Uh . . .

Will Campbell: What troubles me is what an emphasis on belief does to discipleship. It negates discipleship, really. Discipleship is the struggle to be like Christ, even though I know I am not Christ and that I am not going to be like Christ perfectly. But I am expected to try. Once I make what I *believe* the issue, then I'm off the hook. I either believe your particular creed or I don't.

Bill McNabb: So belief becomes a substitute for action?

Will Campbell: Right. So I don't care about how you live, what I care about is whether you believe in the infallibility of Scripture.

Bill McNabb: Oh great, you *would* have to bring that subject up.

Will Campbell: Infallibility?

Bill McNabb: Well, yes.

Will Campbell: To be quite honest with you, I never have understood that issue. *No one* believes the Bible literally. No one. Pat Robertson, Judge Pressler, Billy Graham—*no one* believes the Bible literally.

Bill McNabb: Don't feel like you have to hold back.

Will Campbell: A fellow came by my house a few years ago and I asked him, "Do you believe the Bible literally?" He responded, "Yes sir, my brother, word for word." I said, "Well, fantastic." I stood up, gave him a courtly bow and ceremoniously got my hat and cane, extended my hand and said, "I didn't know there was anyone else in the world who believed the way I do. The Bible says that the day has come to proclaim the opening of the doors of the prison and letting the captives go free. I've been looking for years to find someone who agreed with the literal interpretation of that scripture 'cause there's this prison over in west Nashville and I can't tear the thing down myself, but if there's 15 million folks out there who believe in the literal interpretation of Scripture, we can get 'em all together and raze that prison to the ground." He looked at me kinda funny and said, "Well, now, what Jesus meant by that was . . ." I shouted, "Don't you go exegeting on *me*." He said he believed in Scripture literally. But the prison's still standing.

Bill McNabb: We all interpret the Scripture.

Will Campbell: It all gets back to what we've been talking about. The futility of fighting over what we believe. What does it matter what someone believes? If you are bringing Good News to the poor and restoring sight to the blind and healing the broken-hearted and releasing the captives, but you happen to believe that a whale swallowed Jonah or you happen *not* to believe that a whale swallowed Jonah, what difference does it make "as long as Christ is preached"?

Bill McNabb: Sounds familiar.

Will Campbell: It does, doesn't it?

Will Campbell

Frye Gaillard / 1997

From *Oxford American*, issue 19 (Winter 1997). Reprinted with permission of Frye Gaillard, writer in residence at the University of South Alabama.

Frye Gaillard: What led you to write about Duncan Gray?

Will Campbell: There are few heroes left in America. Duncan Gray Jr. is one of mine. He's such an exceedingly modest, unassuming character, almost meek, and yet, on the night of the riot with a dangerous, exploding mob—two people shot dead—here was this fellow with his turned-around collar climbing up on the Confederate monument, pleading for calm. When I asked his wife where he got this courage, she said, "Will, that's just what a priest does. That morning he administered the sacraments during service at the church. That was part of his job. And when there is trouble, a priest is a peacemaker. That's a part of his job also."

Frye Gaillard: In your book, you weave Duncan Gray's story through the story of a group of young men from Ole Miss who left their studies to go fight in the Civil War. Talk about the connection—how in your mind the two stories are related.

Will Campbell: I was struck by the irony of history. Company A of the Eleventh Mississippi Infantry Regiment became known as the Mississippi Greys. That name—Grey with an E—was one letter different from Duncan Gray's, and when they stacked their books and went off to war, their point of departure was precisely the place where Gray with an A pleaded for calm during the riots at Ole Miss. The Mississippi Greys never came home. Not a one of them. They sustained 100 percent casualties at the Battle of Gettysburg, which has been called the high-water mark of the Confederacy. Everyone knew after that how the war was going to end. Everyone knew the Confederacy was doomed and, with it, the institution of slavery. And when Duncan Gray went around and asked for the guns and the gasoline to be put aside, the Molotov cocktails, the rioting that he was trying to stop was the high-water mark of massive resistance to *Brown v. Board of Education*, the landmark case for desegregation. The next week, the businesspeople of Mississippi, the same people who had put Governor Ross Barnett in office and given their tacit approval to resistance, issued a statement saying that compliance with *Brown v. Board* must be done. They said, "We will not allow violence to be the means of conflict." So I was writing about those two high-water marks in our struggle with what Gunnar Myrdal called "the American Dilemma," the issue of race.

Frye Gaillard: Have the waters receded where the racial issue is concerned?
Will Campbell: It depends on which day you ask me that question. I cannot agree with those who say things are no better than they were in 1954. What some of the people, who say that, are seeing is that black Americans are now free to state their grievances and to strike back, sometimes even physically. "Why are they so angry?" That's the question you hear, and it's always "they." But black Americans are no more angry today than they have ever been. The difference is, they can now talk back, or yell back if they want to, where fifty years ago it would have led to a lynch mob.

Frye Gaillard: In your work as a Southern Baptist minister, a renegade preacher in many people's eyes, you have made the connection, as Duncan Gray did, between faith and the issue of race. What do you think made you see that connection?
Will Campbell: There were a number of things. There was the time when I was five years old and this elderly black man came by my house. I was playing with a group of my cousins, and we were taunting him, calling him "nigger." Our granddaddy called us over, and he told us, "There ain't no niggers in this world. That's a colored *man*," and he emphasized the word *man*. That had a profound impact on me. Why it didn't affect my cousins, I don't know. I was no smarter than they were, no more sensitive or pious, so I can't answer that. Then, during World War II, I was in the Pacific and there were dark-skinned natives who would sometimes come to the hospital where I was working. One of them, who was working as a servant for a white man, had been kicked in the spleen for dropping an ashtray. I got to thinking about things in Mississippi, and I said to myself, this kind of cruelty sounds vaguely familiar. I started reading about the issue, and at that point it was not a Christian thing, until I did some more study and I made that connection. Duncan Gray made it right away—from the very beginning. He

believed in the radical nature of the liturgy: if you eat this bread and drink this wine, it's supposed to mean something.

Frye Gaillard: When you compare Duncan Gray's Christian witness with some of the TV ministers we are seeing today, how does that make you feel?
Will Campbell: I feel almost ill. We are big today on a kind of feel-good spirituality. But I believe, and Duncan Gray believes, that anything that does not lead you to the streets—into the world—for the betterment of God's world is fraudulent. It's phony. A friend of mine was talking to me this morning, telling me about an event here in Nashville. There were fifteen thousand people in the city arena being healed by a TV evangelist. My friend said, "Will, why didn't this minster, this healer, just go over to the hospital? That's where the sick people are."

Frye Gaillard: Is there one issue that grows out of your faith that stands out above all the others?
Will Campbell: Race is important. It's been our great dilemma in this country. But this book I have written is a book about grace. It's a sermon really. There are some stories in it that I think are interesting—a group of young men going to war, a priest who stands against the troubles of his time. But it's a book about grace, the divine forgiveness that rains down upon all us. Duncan Gray understands that in a more profound sense than anyone I have ever known: we are forgiven—everyone for everything. As the book ends, I am visiting a place in Mississippi called Sullivan's Hollow, the most remote place I've ever been in, and I'm walking side by side with the Imperial Wizard of the Ku Klux Klan. I had talked to many of Duncan Gray's friends, but I had talked to none of his enemies, and there were reports that Duncan had been marked by the Klan for execution. I was never able to verify that, but I wanted to talk to someone that I knew had differed with him strongly. As we were talking and driving around, this man from the Klan had asked to stop at a cemetery, a place in the woods down a tiny dirt road. He took his place at the foot of the grave and he called the man's name who was buried there. He said, "I am not presuming anything, but if your spirit is lingering, I want you to know that I still miss you. I love you." His voice trailed off and he began to weep. As we walked away he said of the man who was buried in the grave. "He was a dear friend, and a staunch Tri-Kappa." It was as if he was equating the KKK with a college fraternity, and he probably was. The thought began to occur to me that what Duncan Gray had been saying all along was that all of us are equals in the eyes of God. He and the Klansman

stood on equal footing before the Deity. That was his radical definition of grace. We are already forgiven, already reconciled to God, and what the liturgy is about is celebrating the mystery of this with thanksgiving.

There are people who are uncomfortable with that definition of grace. If everyone is forgiven for everything they do—if a Klansman is forgiven for his message of hate—doesn't that count as license to continue with business as usual?

It does not amount to license. Once this notion of grace breaks through, it has implications for the way we live. If I have a parent so good, so accepting of me and my frailty, I can't take that as license to go on kicking that parent in the teeth. I see Christian worship as a way of being thankful. But if our worship does not lead us into good works, it is a sham.

Interview #21

Mike Letcher / 2000

From *God's Will*, 2000. 2775 Interview #21, 81–85. University of Alabama Center for Public TV & Radio, Mike Letcher, producer, https://vimeo.com/55126898. Reprinted with permission of the producer.

Mike Letcher: How is your writing related to what you see as your ministry?

Will Campbell: My writing is my soapbox. I guess. My pulpit. You know, I either wasn't ready for the pulpit and the steeples or they weren't ready for me, but it didn't work. I've always liked to write. And I started writing when I was a very small boy. I was always the runt. I don't always look like it now, but I was. And we'd go out to play ball on Saturday and Sunday afternoons. And I'd be invariably and apparently inevitably that last one to be chosen, and that always hurt my feelings, so I wouldn't go out. I'd stay in the house and write cowboy stories, which was all I had ever read except the Bible, and I was pretty sure I couldn't improve on that at that time. Then when I didn't make it in the steeples, I started writing rather regularly. Writing is my voice box. Although I'm not aware of that when I write a book. When you get a certain age, people start analyzing your work, deconstruction and all that business. And I'm not consciously up to anything. But I know it comes out of who I am. It comes from somewhere. Some guy said everything Campbell has ever written has been about the search for community. And I would agree to that. I wasn't aware of it at the time. *Brother to a Dragonfly* was the search between Joe, my brother, and myself in the larger context. And *The Glad River* was the three guys who called themselves "the community" or neighborhood. So that's what my writing is. It's my pulpit. And it's a limited one because I'm not a John Grisham writer. I couldn't be if I wanted to be, I've never tried to do that kind of writing. But if I may be immodest, there are maybe twenty thousand people out there who read what Campbell writes, and whether it influences them or not is not for me to say. That's enough to satisfy any ego need that I might have for a following. And we all have those needs of course. But that's not a bad pulpit—I'm not saying that, you know, they read Campbell every week the way some people would listen to their Sunday eleven o'clock preacher. But that's what it's about.

Mike Letcher: Your writings before *Dragonfly* were directed toward the religious community There were two books and the magazine, *Katallagete*?
Will Campbell: The magazine that I published for a number of years was called *Katallagete*. A lot of people thought that was rather presumptuous for a little bunch of southern rednecks—publish and edit a magazine with the fancy Greek name, but that's precisely why we named it that. Show them we know some Greek, too.

Mike Letcher: Was there a mission statement for that group and that magazine?
Will Campbell: It was in a sense a kind of interpretation or exegesis of that passage in which the word, *katallagete*, is used. To BE what you are already. That is all race relations are about. We're not having conferences and next steps and light at the end of the tunnel and all the touchy feely things that to some groups that might be ever so efficacious, but that wasn't what we were about. And we were addressing ourselves to the Christian community with the clear understanding, of course, that Christians are not the only ones who are interested in reconciliation. In fact, unfortunately, Christians in America are in many respects less interested in reconciliation than the Jewish community, because of history. The Christian community has never suffered the persecution that the Jewish community has experienced and witnessed. But, we were saying that if we behaved, according to our nature that alone would solve the problem of race. Race would cease to exist and would have absolutely no meaning. And I think the magazine served a purpose during a period when we were, of course, criticizing the liberal community, which was criticizing ourselves, because we fit in that, too, you know.

And I had an interesting experience recently. I was in another state and a man came over to my table at a restaurant and started saying some very flattering things about me and my writing and so on. And after a while, I asked him, "What do you do?" and he said, "I'm a state supreme court justice." And I flinched. And I asked, "How long have you done that?" And he said, "Just since about four months ago." And so it dawned on me that he had been appointed by a very right-wing Republican governor. And he kept talking about "you converted me, you turned my life around," and I couldn't figure that out until it dawned on me later that he would have been a young student during the Vietnam War when we were being so critical of Johnson and Kennedy. That was after all, their war. It wasn't Nixon's war. We were saying that politics is an illusion. The influence of that crazy Frenchman, Jacques Alue, and it is an illusion. But what he was reading was, "Well, if these guys are attacking liberal democratic politics, because of the war and other things, then what that means is you must become right-wing Republican," which is quite the opposite of what we were trying to say. If politics is an illusion, then ALL politics is an illusion. And of course, our message was "politics as messiah is a false messiah and it leads you down the road to ruin," which it does in my judgment. I forgot what your question was, but that's the answer.

Mike Letcher: The beginnings of your broader writing career, like your return to your roots, was triggered by a tragic event. What was the relation between the writing of *Dragonfly* and Joe's death?

Will Campbell: I don't know really. When I wrote the book, I didn't write it immediately after my brother's death. It was probably a year before I could really come to grips with it. But I wrote it in just a brief period of time. And I didn't have in mind writing a book for publication. I didn't write it to publish. I wasn't thinking this was a catharsis though it probably was, and I didn't do anything with it until seven years later, I think. A publisher asked me if I would write a book for his company, his house on personal theology. And I didn't know what that meant. Still don't. And I said, "No, I don't think so." And he said, "Well do you have anything you would like to write?" And I said, "Well, I have this manuscript if you want to look at it." Well, of course, I went back and did some more work on it to write it as a publishable book as it came to me. But I think, no one enjoys the tragedy. But until you do come to grips with tragedy, I think, you're not a whole person. And a lot of people simply refuse to acknowledge the tragedy of human existence itself. Joe was a good man. And so his story was in a real sense a tragedy in the Greek sense of tragedy. Everyone is trying to do the right thing, and is doing the right thing according to their best knowledge and information. But things still don't turn out right.

And I think the same thing about the South and the suffering of the South—black and white, the Civil War, Reconstruction, all the rest. Now that may be a metaphor which no one but me would understand, but I think it's true. And I'm a big, what Tom T. Hall calls part of the "metaphorical mafia," you know, as we call ourselves. But you're right, you know. I've written, what, I think sixteen books now. That was kicked off really by that tragedy—I had done some other things—but it's the kind of thing that anyone with a job may do, you know—sort of trade books in a sense. Even *Race and Renewal of the Church* was a subject that was very important to me, but it was part of my job, part of my work to write this sort of thing, whereas the other things have been freelance. It's just something that's inside me that must come out somehow. And it makes its way out the tip of my finger on a typewriter.

Mike Letcher: Can you elaborate on the idea of Joe as a metaphor for the South?

Will Campbell: Well Joe's very existence was threatened. And his personal life, his marriage, and so on. And he turned to amphetamines. He was a pharmacist. It was very easy. There was no such word as "speed" at the time. It was just a respectable pharmaceutical that he could reach for up on his shelf and get to help him through the day and through facing trying times at home and so on. It was a metaphor in the sense that the South faced very trying days, and turned to something. Joe turned to something for comfort that let him down. The South, the white South turned to something following the Civil War that also let it down—segregation. There was really no need for segregation following the Civil War. But because we were a tragic people and a hurt people and a defeated people as Joe was hurting and defeated in so many ways. We said, "Well, we may be whipped and we may be this and that and the other, but we're white and we will set ourselves apart and we will establish this institution of segregation that will deliver us."

But it never did deliver us. Far from it, it proved to be our undoing. If we had, if the church, for example, had not—see, the church prior to the Civil War was not segregated. My little Baptist church in the rural most southern part of Mississippi, the most southern, southwestern part of Mississippi, the blacks and whites worshipped together until the Civil War. Now I understand why they separated. Segregation was going to deliver us from the defeat and from the hurt sting of being humiliated. Well, we were beaten. The Yankees whipped us and stripped us of our wealth, which was considerable. Mississippi was the wealthiest state in the Union, with all these millionaires and so on. But we're white. And we bet on that horse, and it let us down. We will have a segregated culture. And that will deliver us from the hurt—just as Joe said, "I will have this little pharmaceutical that I can pull down off my shelf to deliver me from my pain." And it did for a long time, but it was the wrong horse to bet on. And segregation was the wrong horse.

And I've long thought that in my little home church, my father was a custodian of the records. They were all black and white in my church. They had no balcony. Some of the urban, city churches would have slave balconies. But, you know, people just sat down there together, slaves and the free people. Now when the war ended, it was not the fault of either race. More the fault, however, of the whites than of blacks, than of the freed men and freed women. They, naturally, wanted to have more leadership. And the whites, naturally, didn't want to grant them more leadership. So more and more, they pulled out and formed their own churches. Now, if—and this is a big if—the church had managed to stay as a nonracial institution, I think it would have made a great deal of difference. In that, we would not have had segregated schools for very long. People would start thinking, particularly when they got their tax bill, "Well, my God, we can't afford one school system, let alone two. This doesn't make any sense. Our children go to Sunday school, black and white together. And they play together, you know, and they have their parties together. Why can't they go to school together?" And people would say, "Well, sure. Why not? That's just ridiculous." So, there would have been no need for *Brown v. Board*, and there would have been no need for what we call the civil rights movement, and I'm sitting here just working out this whole thing beautifully.

But I think that's true. If the church had been faithful to what it was, since Pentecost, it would have been the salt. It would have been the leavening in the lump. But it didn't. It denied the faith. And it segregated itself more rigidly than any other institution and culture. And it still is more rigidly segregated than any other institution and culture, though it's trying, but it's failing. And maybe the failure itself is the judgment that simply waited too late. And what do you do when you're under judgment? Try not to cry out.

Mike Letcher: How are the themes of reconciliation and freedom played out in *Brother to a Dragonfly*, in particular?
Will Campbell: Well, I think the whole thing—the community in *Brother to a Dragonfly*—and when I say "community," it doesn't have to be vast hordes, the community Joe and I were seeking. You remember the scene where Joe was getting married and he said we're going to have a bachelor party, just the two of us, no one else is invited? And he had two little bottles of Four Roses whiskey there. And he put one down in front of each of us. And he drank his and I didn't? And Joe was crushed by that, and sad? He got, you know, mildly in the grape before the evening was over and said, "Will, why didn't you come to my party?" You know, that kind of search for unity and

community and I rebuffed him. And it was nothing conscious about it. I wasn't saying, "Well I'm not going to sit here and have a drink with you." It wasn't that at all. It was an unconscious thing. But it was a rebuff. I didn't come to his party, you know. And he was going through all of that in this mild—you know, he wasn't roaring drunk or anything like that. He was reminiscing about our early childhood and all those things and just reaching out and crying out for me to embrace him—to join in this festivity. And I was, you know, thinking about tomorrow or whatever. When I had to be up there, stand up in my robe in this rich Calvinist Birmingham church and say pretty words. Even then, you know, he accepted me. Joe was the real, Joe was the real tragedy and the real community seeker and community provider, far more than I was, far more than I. And that's something that I've never really emotionally recovered from—I know that I feel a responsibility for Joe in many ways. Again, that's the nature of tragedy. I didn't mean to do it. I thought, "Well, what you do to Joe is, when he needs money, give him money or whatever." But the emotional need for acceptance and for—for community—I know of no other word. That need was there, and I didn't provide it.

. . . And who knows? That may be the thing that has spurred me all these years to be involved in the search for community on a broader level. Maybe this is deep down in me, trying to make up for this early failure. I don't know. I've never been to a psychiatrist, but that's something that he might like to toy with, if I wanted to expose my head to him or her, which I don't have any intention of doing.

There are a lot of little things we can do. I think it's inexcusable that every white person does not, and this sounds artificial—does not make friends with a person of another race.

[This last question is an excerpt from Interview 24, a later segment in the documentary, and is added here by permission. —Editor's Note]
Mike Letcher: Do you ever think that your life of example might spread and have a wide impact?
Will Campbell: Of course we're all propagandists in a sense. Anyone who writes. Even if it's—some would say, "Well, I'm just trying to entertain them." Well. That's influencing behavior. Enjoying something is behavior. . . . Certainly you would hope you are influencing them. That's not for me to say. . . . That's something that troubles a lot of people. It doesn't trouble me so much. It did at one point. . . . Who will tell the stories? In other words, if there's not an institutional church, then in a generation or two the Christian

faith or the Jewish faith, or whatever, will disappear. Because they have not heard the stories. And the scripture says, when the children ask, "What meaneth these stones?" And whose gonna answer what these stones mean? The steeples. The icons and so on. What's the meaning of this? A couple of things. One is that's a very poor doctrine of the Holy Spirit. That if this is supposed to survive, it will. Somehow.

I see it in music. Had a young fellow come here. Turned out he was a second cousin of mine. He didn't grow up in the church. Grew up pretty much on the streets of New Orleans. And he's a young songwriter and he wrote a song called "Good Friday Morning," which is really a summary of the whole Christian gospel. Now, how did he know that? I don't know. But the stories will be told. . . .

We, I think, are all ceremonialists at heart. I am. We're ritualists at heart. We want the ceremonial, the pageantry, and all that. And that's one of the things I miss in the institutional church. But I think it does go on. And this is something difficult to talk about because it sounds as if one is saying, "I can do this better than the institutional church." I can't. There are some things here in this cabin that are sacramental. Not just ceremonial or ritualistic. But sacramental.

Sacramental in the biblical sense of the word. For example, a man came here. A lawyer from a large city. He was a friend of mine and he said, "I want you to baptize me." I've never been baptized and I'm attending an Episcopal church. A cathedral. And, as it happened—I don't mind mentioning the church—it's St. Andrew's Cathedral in Jackson, Mississippi. And I had known this man for some time. He's actually a member of our little group called "the brotherhood," our writers group.

And he said, "I used to be a Baptist." I said, "Well, if you used to be a Baptist, you don't need baptizing." He said, "No, I haven't. Just take my word for it, I haven't been baptized. But I'm now going to the Episcopal church and I like to sing in the choir. And I want to be baptized. And I want to be a member."

Well, as it happened, I knew the dean or the rector of that church. And I called him and he said, "Yeah, I know, Will, what you're talking about. And we've discussed, my position is that the community that's going to sustain one should be the one to baptize them." And it makes a lot of sense. And I said, "Well now, look, I agree with that, but he's already said to me, 'Look, you guys are my community. You've sustained me for twenty-five years. You know, we run together. We go places together. We read books together.' And so on and so on." And so I told my friend, the rector of that parish, I said,

"Now, you know, I'm not going to get into that. Whether you accept this baptism is of no consequence to me. I have no interest in that. Whatsoever. But if he comes to my yard and says, 'Will, will you baptize me?' I'm going to baptize him." So that was a bit awkward. So he was up here and Tom T. Hall was here. And Jim Whitehead, a poet—a very fine poet from the University of Arkansas—runs the writers' program there. Whitehead read a poem about Smith County, Mississippi, where this man grew up. I read a passage of scripture. I read a passage from *The Glad River* where my character is baptized in prison. And Tom T. sang *Amazing Grace*. And I asked him, "Are you asking me for the sign?" And he said, "Yes." And you repent of your sins? "Yes." He kneeled down and I poured three dippers of water over his head. From the pot back there behind the cabin. And he was baptized. Well, you've still got the steeples to deal with. This man wanted to be a member in full standing of St. Andrew's Episcopal Cathedral in Jackson, Mississippi. So I'm not above dealing with them. And I'm not above being modestly deceptive.

An Interview with Will D. Campbell

Benjamin Houston / 2003

From *Journal of Southern Religion* 10 (2007). http://jsr.fsu.edu/Volume10/Houston.htm. Reprinted with permission.

Benjamin Houston: It is July 1, 2003. I am in the cabin of Will Campbell near Mount Juliet, Tennessee. Reverend Campbell, I know you were born in Mississippi. What was the date?
Will Campbell: July 18, 1924.

Houston: How would you describe 1950s Nashville to me, an outsider both to Nashville and the 1950s?
Campbell: Nashville was deceiving itself. It thought that it was ahead, and it was, ahead of, say, Jackson, Mississippi, or Birmingham or Montgomery and so on, in terms of some leadership that did not want to be embarrassed by being haters and all that. But underneath that, you had some old aristocracy. The old Fugitive movement [a group of poets at Vanderbilt University], for example, was here. That was a racist movement. Actually, Donald Davidson [Vanderbilt professor of English, Fugitive poet, and Southern Agrarian], who was a fine writer, reporter, and others, I thought they had some good ideas when they talked about, you know, throw the radio out the window and take the banjo and the fiddle down off the wall. I thought that was cool. I still do. But, when it happened, why could not Donald Davidson, and I am using him as a prototype, or even others have said to Uncle Dave Macon and the Grand Ole Opry early-timers, say, hey, man, it would be cool, we will go down to the Ryman Auditorium [site of Grand Ole Opry], and you pick your banjo and you sing me mountain songs, and then I will read poetry. And let there be this fusion of folk and university culture. Instead of that, they moved to Belle Meade [a wealthy and exclusive suburb of Nashville] and didn't read anything but one another's [work]. They were embarrassed by the mountain, the rural people, the country music.

Houston: You have acknowledged that there is a distinction between a place like Nashville and Mississippi, and you would credit that with the leadership in the first place and a certain self-image in Nashville?

Campbell: Partly self-image, plus it wasn't as rural. Of course, I grew up in it, so what I say has to be kind of sifted through that sieve of small-farm yeomen culture. We were not on plantations. We did not work with other people, blacks and others. We did the work ourselves. . . . So, it was definitely a different culture from what I had grown up in.

Houston: Talk a little bit about how you came to be involved with the Tennessee Council on Human Relations.

Campbell: Well, that was not my major organization. I was involved in it. But I came to Tennessee in 1955. I was for all practical purposes kicked out of the University of Mississippi, where I was director of religious life, and that is another story that has nothing to do with Nashville, really, except that I wound up here. With the National Council of Churches, it was a new ingredient in Nashville culture. They had never had any staff-people here. It was very suspect even by [the standards of] some of the more enlightened churches. But being left-wing, if they'd only known how powerless it was, you know, they wouldn't have fooled with it. But we were small in number, the "liberal organizations."

That is how I first got to know George Barrett [Nashville attorney]. He was a law student living most of the time with his grandma. He's a Nashvillian. His daddy worked at the Jarman Shoe Company, or when they could get a job, although there was a vicious anti-Irish feeling here. He went to Father Ryan High School. When they would play other schools, they [people at the other high schools] would throw fish out on the court and all kind of stuff. So, he grew up with some real prejudice directed at him. But he was a young fellow, and then he went off to England for a year and came back and then was a young lawyer here. He was interested in "liberal causes," and was a labor lawyer primarily then. Of course, he has done a lot of things. George made a lot of money. I have a son who is a lawyer, and he is making a lot, too. I never made any, but that is okay. I have made all I needed. I have got sixty acres of woods here, my old cabin, and a good wife. What else is there?

But the Tennessee Council on Human Relations was, I think, not even in existence at that time. I don't recall when it was founded. But the Southern Regional Council got hold of some money, I am not sure if it was Ford [Foundation] money, but a whole passel of money to start councils in each state in the South. I was active in the little movement here. I knew about this guy in Dallas, Texas, a Methodist preacher named Baxton Bryant. I called him Booger Red because [of his] big red hair. He was a wild man. He had run for Congress against a very conservative Dallas congressman back in the 1950s. He ran against him twice and came within ninety-seven votes of beating him one time on a pro-labor, pro-civil rights ticket, but he didn't. So I had him come over here, and he was interviewed, and he kind of took it.

But before that, there was a group, made up primarily of women, who, during the sit-ins in 1960 and earlier, they were standing around watching. They would go to court. It was almost like South Africa. They sat in the courtroom and observed what was going on and observed the violence. I will never forget, in February of 1960 when the first sit-in here was taking place. This is wandering around from your question, but it all gets back to it eventually, maybe.

There was an awful lot of violence. The degree of violence in Nashville has never really been told. . . . Anyway, my job was to be an observer. I wasn't one of the participants who had been trained by Rev. James M. Lawson. You will no doubt run into that name many times, and I hope, certainly, that you can interview him at some point.

Houston: Me, too.

Campbell: Because he was a driving force in the Nashville student movement, which involved the adults later on. He got them as involved as they were. . . . First Baptist Capitol Hill was a black church. I was a member, but I think I was the only white member. That was where the kids were meeting, and they would come out in groups of forty, thirty, or whatever the number was, up to the Woolworth's store and Kreske's and one other store. Word got around. It was a snowy Saturday morning and afternoon, and as soon as they would be seated and turned away, they would be arrested, taken to jail, and they were filling the jails.

Upstairs, there was a smaller lunch counter, but there was more violence up there. As I recall, they were all male students sitting in up there. Downstairs, they were male and female. But this mob would come in, and they would spit on the kids and pull their hair and try to jerk them off [the stools]. There was this elderly woman. I did not know who she was. She would go up and down the line. She would see somebody spit on a girl or jerk her hair, and she would single them out and say something like, "Now, you look like a nice young man. I bet you have a sweet little sister at home. How would you feel if that was your sister?" And the guy, generally, didn't know how to answer.

It was a mob scene. They weren't organized. Individuals [harassing civil rights protesters] would lose face, and would drop out. Then somebody else would take over. . . . I am convinced that this old woman singlehandedly kept [the peace], because at one point, the police pulled out and just left the kids at the mercy of the mob. Because I was white and had some contacts at city hall, I could, by subterfuge, generally, find out when the strategy would change. One hour, it would be arrest them all as soon as they were seated, arrest them and put them in the paddy wagon. Well, that didn't work. That did not scare them because they kept coming, kept coming, kept coming. Finally, the word was, pull all the police out and lock the doors. That is what happened while this old woman was pretty much singlehandedly keeping the peace.

Upstairs, I watched this one guy built like [the boxer] Mike Tyson, a black guy, and I said, that guy is about to lose his cool. A fellow came in, a white guy with a big old pointed cap and a feather, and they called him Old Green Hat, like Robin Hood, you know. He was a leader, and he took over, and he was trying to jerk this guy off the counter seat and finally did jerk him off [the seat]. And I heard a [swish], like a switch-blade knife. I never saw the knife, I never knew who had it, but out of the crowd came this white guy, preppie-looking fellow, we would call him today, and he grabbed this guy and said, "You son of a bitch, if you touch him again, I'll stomp the piss out of you." Old Green Hat said, "Hey, here come the cops." Well, there were no cops, but Old Green Hat had lost face.

This woman down there who was just watching turned out to be a member of the Methodist Sunday School Board. [She] told me, "I came down here to buy an egg poacher," and said, "I am not going to stand there and see these poor little girls treated like that, so I just did what [I could do]." She didn't see it as a heroic [thing to do]. But they would go to court and sit and testify about what they had observed and so on.

Houston: Were they part of the United Church Women or the Tennessee Council?

Campbell: There were United Church Women. If there was an organization that they could claim, most of them would have been involved somehow in United Church Women. But a lot of it was the Tennessee Council on Human Relations.

Houston: Since you brought up Baxton Bryant, could you talk a little bit more about him? I know as it got later into the 1960s, he ended up being a very controversial figure.

Campbell: It depends on who you talk to as to how controversial he was. He was a wild man and wasn't scared of the devil. He and George Barrett had their differences, and George and I know that. We have talked about it, and I have kidded George about it. I said, "You were scared of Baxton." George would reply, "I wasn't scared of that son of a bitch. He was crazy." Well, he wasn't crazy, but he did like to be on the cutting edge. He wanted to be put in jail and was. I don't think he was ever put in jail here, but down in Fayette County, Tennessee, in that movement there, he went to jail. Yes, he was an important player. By the time he came along, the Tennessee Council had moved from this more sedate and politically sophisticated [movement and] more into a revolutionary-type movement. It had more young people in it. That was down Baxton's alley. That is what he wanted to lead, and did lead. He had a sizable following. Now, it was about that time that money began to run out and all the state councils actually died.

But the Tennessee Council on Human Relations would have been rated in terms of effectiveness or in terms of action between the militancy of the young people's movement, the student movement, or SNCC as it was called after 1960, when it was organized in Raleigh, North Carolina. And Nashville was probably the most important representation at that meeting [at Shaw University] in Raleigh, there and Virginia Union, I believe was the name of that college. There was real competition about who was going to run this new student organization, and finally Nashville prevailed.

Houston: Some people I have talked to have sort of insinuated, and it sounded like you made overtones of this, that in the late 1950s, maybe the Tennessee Council was more of a social group in the sense of an interracial social group . . . tea parties and conversation and that sort of thing. Would you agree with that assessment?

Campbell: Well, I think the word tea party is a little off, but it did not have the militancy of SNCC, for example. These were people like Louise Young, who taught at Scarritt College, a Methodist school here, and Kay Jones, who was a social worker. Then you had people at Fisk, people like Vivian Henderson, who taught political science, very urbane, very sophisticated. He was appalled when SNCC came along, you know. It wasn't that he disapproved of it. It was just, man, "I didn't think my people had those kind of guts. I have been thinking about doing this, you know, being militant like this, all of my life." So, that is what the Tennessee Council was. It went back, actually, to something that I had worked [with] for a time. I left the National Council of Churches for something called the Committee for Southern Churchmen, which was an offshoot of the old Fellowship of

Southern Churches, which you will no doubt run into. There was a fairly strong chapter here in Nashville.

Houston: That brings up an important question. How would you character-ize the race relations within these interracial groups like the Committee of Southern Churchmen and the Tennessee Council? How did those dynamics work? Were there vestiges of southern paternalism, even among liberals and moderates?

Campbell: Oh, sure. There was that, and there was a kind of timidity. . . . It certainly was part of the long progression there that gradually developed. Race relations in the South and, I think, in America, have always operated like a sieve. A certain crisis, like the First World War, for example, would change things and it would open up a little bit, and more blacks and other minorities would come through to the main culture, but then it would con-strict again. The pressure would come along, and the whites would say, "To hell with the niggers." Not that it was just the war that would open the net, the mesh, but that more than anything else did so. Then the Second World War occurred. Black soldiers went ahead and did fight and did die and then came back, and it was the same old crap going on. Then it opened up a little bit more, and the majority culture, being the white culture, allowed it to open a little bit more but not enough. Just some.

Houston: So, even these people who are justly celebrated for doing this interracial work, like in the Tennessee Council, they still were slowly evolv-ing in their own racial attitudes, to a certain extent.

Campbell: Oh, sure. Yes, I think we all were. My personal feeling is, my conversion was almost instantaneous in the Second World War. I mean, I grew up in Mississippi, although my father was not a bigot and his father was not. I do not know why. My mother was very much so. But my grandfa-ther, I remember once, he was a man who could read and write, but that was about the extent of it. We would always meet down at his house, all the little grandchildren, on Sunday afternoon to play. We were taunting an old black man who recently had been released from prison for stealing [some] corn out of a white man's field and sent to the penitentiary for it. He was shuffling off down the road, not looking at anything around, and we were saying, "Hi, nigger, hi, nigger." Grandpa called us all around and said, "Now, you don't do that. There are no niggers in the world." We replied, "Yeah, Grandpa, yon walking, he's a nigger." "No, he is a colored man," which was the accept-able, proper designation. He was a man. I never forgot that. Now, I am not saying that was some kind of a Damascus Road experience for me, nor can I explain—there must have been twelve or fifteen of us there, all boys—why most of the rest stayed on and joined the White Citizens' Council and, some of them, even more violent organizations than that. I mean, there was this period of about twelve or fifteen years—this is kind of wandering away from Nashville, but you asked about my evolution—when I could not go home. I would have been killed.

There was a family reunion every year, a big one. My daddy, for about eight or ten years, he never mentioned it, but I knew that it met every year on the last Sunday of May. Up to that time, he would always say, "Well, I will see you the last Sunday in May." And, yes, I would be there. . . . Then, one day we were talking, and my father said, "Well, I guess I will see you Sunday." "Well, I don't know, Dad; what's the temperature down there?" He said, "Now that's all over." He said, "Now, you might hear in people's private homes from Friday at 5:00 to 8:00 Monday morning, people saying 'nigger,' but come 8:00 Monday morning, it is 'Mr. Robbins,' because everyone is working for one federal program or another where they can't get away with that kind of talk." You know, when you are young, which you are, you don't think you are ever going to die or be killed by a bunch of racists. You know, I was born to live forever. So, I did not take it that seriously. But one or two times, Daddy made use of my brother Joe, who kind of protected me. I don't know if you know about Joe.

Houston: I have read about him.

Campbell: A great American. He would keep me informed on when it was safe, when it wasn't safe, and so on. He called me a couple of times and said, "Don't go home this summer or this month" or whatever.

There was one old boy I grew up with down there, and he was my best buddy. He was a little older and was a little bit below our class level. He dropped out of school about the seventh or eighth grade. We were pals. We would carve our initials in blood. You know, we were blood brothers and all. Just before he died—he died of emphysema—I had stopped at the little single-wide trailer where he was living down there. I had been to see my parents. We called him Hog. I said, "Hog, how close did I come?" He said, "Dave [Reverend Campbell's middle name], we were wrong to think that a few of us down here could hold off the United States Army, the Supreme Court, the Congress, the National Guard, and we were going to say you can't do this." He said, "Now, I was with them when we were looking for you, but I wasn't going to let them kill you. Now, we were going to have an understanding, but I was armed, and then I was going to say, 'okay, boys, that is enough.'" Well, I said, "Now the only trouble with that, Hog, you take me down to Homichitti Bottoms and beat the hell out of me or whatever you do to exact this understanding, and then you say, 'turn him loose.' I knew all of you. Most of you were kin to me, had gone to school with me. Even if you had masks on, I knew you. But you didn't know me. You didn't know what I did. You knew rumors. You didn't know if I was a communist or the head of the FBI in Mississippi. You didn't know what I did, who I represented." I said, "They would have killed me after they had the under-standing, [even if] they would have had to kill you." He said, "Well, Dave, they would have had to kill me." I don't know if that is southern, and I don't want to be sexist about it, whether it was the southern boys' loyalty or what it was, but there is something there that he would have said, "No, if you come by me to get to him, you are going to fall dead." That fortunately did not happen because I did not go there. That was one of the times Joe called and said, "Daddy said don't come home this weekend." I don't know how we got off [track]. I don't think that is the answer to your question.

Houston: That is something, though. That is quite a story. Let me ask this: How did the groups like the Tennessee Council coexist with the other groups, both predominantly white and the black civil rights groups in the 1950s and 1960s, like the Committee of Southern Churchmen, for example?
Campbell: They were supportive. They were support groups. I was a part of the Tennessee Council on Human Relations, and I was also a member of the NAACP, but I wasn't active in the NAACP. Very few white people were. A few. Some people like Nelson and Marion Fuson, for example, who taught at Fisk University, would have been active in the NAACP. I simply joined just because I could. When I was in Mississippi, it would have been, well . . .

Houston: You would have been noticed, I am sure.
Campbell: You wouldn't have survived at that time. When I was at Ole Miss, the state legislature passed a law, I guess, that everyone who was on the staff or faculty at Ole Miss had to sign a document of every organization they had ever belonged to. Well, of course, they were looking for NAACP mem-bers. Anybody would have been a fool to admit that. At that time, I wasn't a member of NAACP. I am not sure there was even a chapter in Oxford at that time, or it was very, very small among blacks, let alone whites. At first, it was such a terrible violation of what I knew as my civil rights. It was none of their business. I put down that I belonged to the Baptist Church and the

Masonic Lodge, I think, two of the safest outfits in the state. I then turned it in. Of course, I did not survive anyway.

Houston: Would you judge the Tennessee Council as an effective organization?

Campbell: I would. At the time, they had inroads into the larger culture and to the press. You had two newspapers here. You had *The Tennessean* that was for the time liberal. It had one whale of a great staff. Then you had *The Banner* that was downright fascist. It later went out of business, not for that reason. Barrett was a little young to have much influence, but he went to work for a fellow named Cecil Branstetter. Cecil had been an old labor lawyer. He was with Bob and all of them, and George. So, George had the input there, and they did have the input on the paper and in the City Club. They could say to the power structure, "Look, you guys shape up; you are embarrassing us; for God's sake, cut this crap out." Now, that did not stop the violence when it came to the sit-ins and desegregating the restaurants and the theaters and so on, but it did set a sort of ethos for people like the mayor, when Diane Nash [Fisk University student who was a key leader in the Nashville student movement] led this group down there. I have seldom seen such a dramatic thing, when she stood there and looked the mayor in the eyes and said, "Do you think it is right"—there were three thousand to five thousand in line behind her—"that we can go in that store and buy anything there, but we can't walk ten feet and get a cup of coffee? Do you think that is right? Do you think it is Christian?" And he started talking about, "Well, my little lady . . ." And she was not a little lady. She was a beautiful young woman, but she wasn't a frail little lady. She said, "Never mind that, Mr. Mayor. Do you think it is Christian?" And he finally said, "No, I don't." When that happened, I knew it was over. I knew that the stores of Nashville would be desegregated.

Now, to touch, at least, on your question. This went all the way back. Now, you couldn't say Louise Young or Kay Jones or Cecil Branstetter ever were directly responsible for this little woman up there asking these questions, an eighteen- or nineteen-year-old kid, but the answer that the mayor finally was forced by her to give was influenced by these people.

Houston: It contributed to the climate.

Campbell: Yes. He knew they were back there, and he personally wasn't a rabid racist. He was, you know, saying, "I am the mayor, and this is what the people elected me to do, and we are going to have segregation here and we are going to have peace and order." So, it does go all the way back, just as the dynamiting of the Hattie Cotton [Elementary] School that night [in September 1957] would go back to a kind of climate of hate.

Houston: A lot of people have said that, in their opinion, the violence at the Hattie Cotton School and then later the bombing of [Z. Alexander] Looby's home drew the battle lines and solidified Nashville's resolution to comply so as to avoid violence. Would you agree with that?

Campbell: I think that was certainly part of it. I don't know that it was the act that solidified it, but more people were changing. . . . Mr. Looby, my God, he was a Republican. He wasn't a dangerous radical. He wasn't American, you know. He was from one of the [Caribbean] Islands. But Avon Williams, who was his partner, worked for him, was very much a Tennessee Negro. But Mr. Looby was a widely respected man, and except for the color of his skin, which was the color of that case there, he would have been president of the Rotary Club or the City Club or whatever. But just because of that, he was in the background, but he was respected, and people, even a lot of the racists, would say, now, "Dynamiting a man's home, you know, that's his castle." That did help some. And the dynamiting of Hattie Cotton School did as well.

But when you start dynamiting schools, well, you are hitting the white folks' pocketbooks. Schools were built with tax funds. And we're not going to let some dumb son of a bitch like John Kasper [itinerant racial demagogue who encouraged violent acts to resist integration in Nashville] come down from the north. In fact, Kasper probably did more to desegregate Nashville than any one person, just by being such a jerk. I don't know whatever became of that fellow, if he went back north or if he died or what happened to him. Then there were a few white preachers who preached hate all the time.

I was, I suppose, more of a liaison between, say, the Tennessee Council and SNCC. So, the Saturday that we were going to sit-in, civil rights workers said, "Call Will Campbell, not to be down there leading, but as a liaison to let us know what is going on in City Hall and among the police." I could mill around and hear what the cops were saying. A few of the cops began to catch on. Just because somebody is a cop, doesn't mean he's stupid. [They would say] what do you do? And I would say, I am a writer, or some partial truth.

Houston: That is actually a perfect segue. Dave Halberstam has written that you had a shrewd sense of how the interior establishment politics of Nashville worked, based on this behind-the-scenes facilitating. Can you elaborate on that? You must have had some sense of the powers that be.

Campbell: We all operate, at least partially or should, within this circum-scribed order . . . within the bounds of some degree of modesty. But it didn't have so much to do with me personally or my own bravery or wit or anything else but it was the color of my skin and my commitment, certainly. [Reverend James] Jim Lawson, who is probably the singularly most influential activist in that period, which was no more than a decade, no more than five or six years, was kicked out or was asked to resign from the Vanderbilt Divinity School. He had been arrested and charged with criminal anarchy because of his lead-ership in the sit-ins. The dean of the Divinity School went over to his home— and they were on friendly terms, and the dean was not a rabid racist but he was representing "The Man"—and Jim gave in. He said, "Don't you think it would be best? Now," he said, "you are going to be expelled, but wouldn't it be better for you to resign?" And then the dean put that in terms of the health of the Divinity School, which Lawson had some feeling about. He was a student there. Jim wasn't an unreasonable person. He said, "Alright, I will do that."

So, together, they wrote a letter. I will never forget. It was snowing, and Jim called me early the next morning and said there was going to be this meeting at 10:00, and "I am going to read this letter of resignation." I said, "Jim, don't leave your apartment until I get there." Now, I have seen this movie; don't do that. They were there. He and [his wife] Dorothy were there when I got over there, over in west Nashville. I said, "Now, Jim, I was in this position at the University of Mississippi, and I did exactly what they are asking you to do, and I was wrong. Now, they were going to kick me out, but I should have made them kick me out so it was a matter of record. You are going to be expelled. You are never going to be able to attend Vanderbilt University, not now. Don't do this."

Now, the dean did not know what my role was, but he came out and he said, "Will, this is doing nobody any good." He said, "It is ruining the name of Vanderbilt Divinity School. The divinity school will never recover from it." Finally, I said, "It is doing nobody good, except the soul of Jim Lawson. He has maintained his integrity." I believed that then and believe it now. Of course, Dean Nelson later changed and was, in effect, fired himself. It was all some interesting days, convoluted and no one progression of events. I am glad I didn't miss it.

Houston: Where do you think that the power was in Nashville, based on your behind-the-scenes understanding? Where were the bases of power in Nashville in terms of running the city? You have insinuated, obviously, that Vanderbilt was a factor. Insurance, as you said earlier.

Campbell: A man who was the chairman of the board of trustees at Vanderbilt University was the publisher of the *Nashville Banner*.

Houston: [James G.] Stahlman.
Campbell: Jimmy Stahlman. He was by far the most powerful man in Nashville. He had allies, certainly, in high places, but that's partly because those allies were the ones who had stock in the *Nashville Banner* and he was beholden to them, the Nashville Life and Accident Insurance Company and so on. The governor at that time [Frank G. Clement], he was a good man who just wanted the controversy to all go away. He did not want protests to be happening, but he knew that he couldn't stop it.

Houston: You have commented elsewhere that politics in Nashville were fairly modern for their time in the 1950s, and yet the social and cultural mentality was much more conservative. Can you elaborate on that dynamic?
Campbell: What was it, ten or twelve, the Fugitives?

Houston: Twelve, the Agrarians.
Campbell: Yes, who were intellectuals, and they were widely respected. People would say, "He is a great poet, he is a great man, a great writer." And they couldn't go on to say, "But he is a bigot. He doesn't like black people, and he doesn't like poor people." That's another thing that troubles me. . . . Whites didn't realize that the very people who were recruiting them for the White Citizens' Council wouldn't wipe their feet on them, and used them only for their cause. That's too bad. I forgot what your question was, but that is the answer.

Houston: There you go. So, there was sort of a distinct reactionary element in Nashville for all of its reputation of moderation.
Campbell: Oh, definitely, yes. Sure.

Houston: This is something that interests me, and I am not sure historians always quite grasp it. Is there such a thing as a thinking segregationist?
Campbell: Yes, I think so. What was I reading just the other day? It was a speech that Lincoln was alleged to have made on the steps of the Capitol, where he was speaking to a black audience right after the Civil War ended. He said, "We have freed you now, but we do not belong together," or something like that.

Houston: You have written about moderation and the fact that, especially as the movement went on, there was perhaps an unfair characterization of moderates in the civil rights movement. Do you still feel that way? . . . If so, how do you look at moderates, especially white moderate southerners now that the movement has progressed over time?

Campbell: I don't really know what the term "moderate" means in terms of race. You either believe that all people are equal or you don't. If you don't, then you are a racist. You are an extremist. If you say, "Well, I believe that we are equal in some ways and some ways we are not," that doesn't makes you a moderate. It makes you a racist. Now, I think I know how people used the word back during the movement. Anybody who said "moderate" meant, "Well, let's don't try to do it overnight." Generally, in my observation, people who said, "Rome wasn't built in a day," they just meant Rome couldn't be built. If you are not going to do it right away, then you weren't going to do it. If you say, "Well, we will do it next year," well, you are an extremist to the people who say never, and there were a lot of people who said never, and still some. I do not know if you were in town the other day. I guess it was a week ago Sunday. Two long articles appeared in the paper about these groups who want to secede, you know, the Southern League. . . .

Houston: I did see that.

Campbell: I don't understand it. That wasn't fit copy. I mean, that ranks right up there with Frank Sutherland's "Wine in Nashville." I get pissed every Monday morning when I open that paper and here is the executive editor of one of the state's leading newspapers and that is his contribution. Not talking about George Bush, not talking about Iraq, but wine in Nashville. Well, I don't give a shit how much wine anybody drinks or what kind. I don't get it.

Houston: Pretty strange, huh?

Campbell: Well, it is childish, except that I understand that the thing is syndicated and it is in a lot of papers. So, if you are in Toledo, well, the heading is "Wine in Toledo." So, here's a guy, well, then just quit being the editor of the *Nashville Tennessean* and let somebody else take the helm. They've got some pretty good journalists down here.

Houston: In terms of Nashville, I was wondering if I could ask you about your insights on the African American perspective of African American Nashvilleans. Could you talk about the generational split that was exhibited by the sit-ins? Did you see a split between the older generation and this newer generation of students?

Campbell: Well, not as much as I anticipated and not as much as I would have thought would have been there. On Monday morning after the Saturday when all the sit-ins took place and all these kids were put in jail—they were all bailed out by Monday night or Tuesday or whatever—I was down at the Citizens' Bank, where I have banked ever since we moved here in 1955. I was down there to borrow some money. I said to the cashier, "Who are all these people in the vaults? He said, "They are bank examiners, federal and state." He said, "I have been a banker for forty-three years or whatever, and I have never had a bank examiner walk in my bank without first making an appointment and telling me they are coming and I have never had state and federal officials do so." He said, "I know what they are looking for, but they are not going to find it. They think that the money that was raised over the weekend to bail these kids out of jail came out of my bank, but it didn't." He said, "Now, you know, they'll find some overdrawn [accounts] and things like that, which you find at any bank in town. They have the right to be back there, so they'll stay all day if they want to."

Houston: So, you think there was actually a high amount of unity between . . .

Campbell: There's no question about it. I know when this *Eyes on the Prize* [civil rights television documentary] [came out], Mrs. Walker, Matthew Walker's mother, appeared to be a funny lady. Her husband is a doctor and very urbane and wealthy, and the kid went to the finest summer camps and all that. He called and said, "Mother, I am in jail." She got tickled. He said, "Be cool, Mother, be cool." She would cry. She would weep, and then she would laugh. Of course, we went down and bailed him out. There was a concerted effort.

Now, there was a lot leading up to that. There were people down at First Baptist Capitol Hill who objected to the church building being used for training because, you know, some of the kids, they would smoke and put out cigarettes on the pews and all that kind of stuff and leave a pretty big mess like young people do, or old ones even do. I think the most telling support for that position I was the Easter boycott. That dried that town up. That brought them to Jesus, I am telling you. The mass meetings at the churches would be packed night after night. You could go to any of the big-name churches, and there, there would be preaching and singing, and there was support from the kids. A few people would say, "Well, the kids are going too fast, and they're just going to get us all in trouble." I was surprised by the support that there was. It was amazing. I was very pleased, because most all of the adults could have said to a seventeen- or eighteen-year-old college freshman, "You cut that out. We don't do that."

Houston: Did you ever get the sense that there were some African Americans in Nashville who maybe were leery of supporting the movement because they had done pretty well for themselves in a segregated society?

Campbell: Oh, sure, no question about that. There were both directions, some because they had done well for themselves and some who hadn't done well, but who didn't want to displease the man. There was an element of Uncle Tomism around, as there always is, still is. Certainly, I couldn't speak for the black masses. My contact was in the movement itself but also in church, and I never heard any . . . Of course, Kelly Miller Smith was the pastor there, and anybody would have been a fool to have said anything against the children, which he called them. We have got to support the children.

Houston: You have talked in an earlier oral history about the image of African Americans in the story of the larger civil rights movement. You have noted that there was almost perhaps an element that raised African Americans to an unrealistic level as these sort of paragons of virtue. Do you recall such comments? I think your remark was, "They were all supposed to look like Lena Horne and be as smart as Ralph Bunche." Can you elaborate on that? I thought that was a really interesting point.

Campbell: Oh, I don't know. It is just an unrealistic expectation that we didn't allow black people to be fully human. They had to either rise above us or they were all black trash, and the truth is not many people are as smart as Ralph Bunche, black or white, or as pretty as Lena Horne. That was, I think, a rationalization, just saying, "Well, they don't act like they are supposed to act." There was an expectation there that, in a sense, did not mean to be racist, but it was. African Americans were supposed to be better than white people, not the same as or even worse.

Houston: Let me stop asking questions for a while and just throw the floor open to you. Is there anything that you feel through your long career in Nashville race relations that hasn't gone explored by historians? You mentioned earlier the element of violence during the sit-ins, but is there anything I should be asking about that I haven't asked about, any details that you wish were recorded by historians that you feel have gone unexamined?

Campbell: Well, maybe there has been, but I have never seen a detailed account of black political activities. See, blacks could vote in Nashville and did vote, but I don't recall there being studies of that. . . . I remember one time, Clifford Allen was running for governor, and George was his big man. I was supposed to be in charge of blacks, you know [laughs]. "I want you to get a dozen or so blacks, and we're going to meet somewhere over in east Nashville," they informed me. We did meet. Clifford Allen came and spoke, and then he left, and so did George. He was trying to organize the black community. He said, "Now, we've got to see this as a mandate, and so next Thursday night, we're all going to meet," and such and such and so. The black person who was kind of the ward healer said, "Now, I hope you understand what this man is saying, that next Thursday night, you fill up your car with mandates and all show up." Of course, George knew better than to laugh out loud, but he said, "What are we getting into? How do you put a mandate in an automobile?" "I don't know. It's your meeting, George."

Houston: Was that pretty common in politics at the time in Nashville?
Campbell: It was fairly common that somebody was going to go after the "black vote," because it was enough to go after. It wasn't a bloc, but it was close to being a bloc. Of course, there weren't as many blacks voting then as there are now, but . . . I don't recall any overt effort to stop them in Nashville, like in my county [Amite County, Mississippi]. There a man was shot dead in front of a cotton gin by a state legislator because he had gone down to register to vote. I don't know if you have seen it, but I have a new little book out about the first black who was elected to state office in Mississippi, Robert George Clark. . . . The title of it is *Robert George Clark's Journey to the House.* I don't like that title, but it's the University Press of Mississippi, and they have to have these academic titles, you know, to sell the academicians. But it is his story, and I think it is a good story. How well I have written it is a different matter. But he has made a difference. Now, some of the SNCC folks and so on, the real militants, felt that he wasn't in your face enough when he was elected, but he knew what he was doing. They had, during the 1950s and 1960s, passed a law repealing the compulsory school law, and he knew the reason for that. He got on the education committee. Then the chairman of the education committee was running for something else, and he was a pretty notorious racist. He came to Robert Clark and said, "Mr. Clark, I lack one vote for Speaker of the House in the legislature. If I had one more vote on my petition . . ." And Clark, who wanted to be on the education committee, knew this would be a way he could get that appointment. He said, "Hand me your pencil." Newman—the guy's name was Newman—got on his knee and said, "I never would have thought that a

peckerwood would get on his knees to a nigger and beg him for his vote in the House of Representatives, but I thank you, sir." And that put him over, and he was Speaker. He then put Clark on the education committee and pretty soon, the chairman got a job in Washington or something and just moved Clark up to be chairman.

Houston: When historians write about the movement, they talk about the integration of schools, voting rights, all those sort of things. What is your sense of how race relations have changed on a day-to-day level among individuals through the 1960s and 1970s and on to now?

Campbell: Personal relationships have changed, for example. We have a friend who is the only black in the subdivision up here close to Lakeside School. We became good buddies and went places together. We would go to eat together and all kind of stuff that we wouldn't have done, even with my changed feeling after I came back from the war. We would have gone different ways when it came lunchtime if we were working on a project together. Now, the families socialize, and nobody thinks anything about it. But there are still white churches and black churches. There are a few blacks in a few white churches and a few whites in a few black churches, but we just waited too late for that. My daddy was custodian of the records of his Baptist church in Mississippi, which was organized in 1808, I believe, when Mississippi was still a territory. Blacks were members of that church. They were listed. T. J. Spurlock and then Alec McCrea. After the war the records would show "FMC," a free man of color, or "FWC," a free woman. Before that it would have been "a slave belonging to . . ." But they didn't have the slave balconies there which you read about because that little old church house was about four times as big as this room. It was just one room, and they all sat together. They were baptized in the same little river down there, the same creek.

Now, after the war, that began to change. My daddy had these records, and I went through them. One of the rules at the church was that if you missed three successive Sundays, you had to go before the church and explain and ask for pardon for being absent. An exception for absence would have been given for a woman in childbirth or if somebody was seriously ill. I noticed more and more and more that at each conference there were fewer FWCs and FMCs. What was happening, these people were going up to Brown's Chapel, a little black church. Now, I understand why they wanted to have their own church. I understand that because they still were not in positions of leadership, for the most part, in the white churches. I have no right to say I expected them to do this, but if they could have held on, then it would not have been too many years before some practical, stingy old planter, who hated paying high taxes, would have said, "Wait a minute, our kids go to [church] together, they swim together, they get baptized together, they go to vacation Bible school together, why we got colored schools and white schools? We can't afford one school system." I think that would have done a lot to break down the pattern of segregation that persisted. But it didn't happen, and I understand, and I don't expect black people to be exempt from Original Sin any more than whites.

Interview with Will D. Campbell

Bob Flynn / 2003

From the *Wittenburg Door Magazine*, November/December 2003. Reprinted with permission of Anthony Ole, publisher, *The Door*.

Will D. Campbell has written some of the most important, most darn readable books from a Christian worldview of the past thirty years, including *Brother to a Dragonfly, Soul among Lions: Musings of a Bootleg Preacher, Forty Acres and a Goat: A Memoir,* and *Providence.* He was also a subject of a couple of unforgettable table interviews with Mike Yaconelli, way back in issue #13 in 1973 and again June/July #110 in 1990. The occasion of this interview is the long-overdue re-release of *The Glad River* by Smyth and Helwys—one of the best novels of any kind in recent memory.

But most importantly, Will D. Campbell is that rarity, a traditional Baptist who knows what that tradition is, who believes scriptural perversion is worse than homosexuality and that greed may be worse than, say, Jack Daniel's, and a gentle iconoclast who happily smashes idols and chains.

You enter his lair—the rustic cabin that serves as office and hide-out—with trepidation and leave the way Jesus's followers must have left: battered, with your idols in shards, your chains dangling and feeling for a little while as if you could fly.

Bob Flynn: Are you pleased that Smyth and Helwys have reprinted *The Glad River*?

Will D. Campbell: Very much so. It was the only one of my books not in print. Most of my books have been in and out of print over the years and, of course, all writers are vain enough to want their offspring to remain in circulation. I was pleased that *The Glad River* is back in circulation because it has always been a personal favorite but wasn't well received when it was originally published. I felt the reviewers didn't understand what I was trying to say. Of course, that's the failure of the writer, not the critic.

Flynn: You think they didn't understand why a young man from Mississippi couldn't find a true Baptist to baptize him in a state where Baptists and Johnson grass are so prevalent?

Campbell: I think that Baptist heritage and history have been so badly waylaid and hijacked in recent years, and so scandalously politicized, that most who call themselves Baptist—I speak here of my own Southern Baptists—have no idea where they came from. Most of those who have taken over the Southern Baptist movement, and are currently making salacious eyes at the American Baptist denomination, haven't the faintest notion of what they looked like three or four hundred years ago in Zurich and Amsterdam and throughout the Low Countries and most of Europe. Now, I know that the line from the Anabaptist to Baptist of the New Country has been a circuitous one, but the best historians have shown that we are kinfolk. Close kin.

Flynn: Any particular historians in mind?

Campbell: Professor William Estep, a great scholar who taught at Southwestern Seminary, that school that once stood tall among theological seminaries but has been taken over by hijackers, proved that there was a nexus. So did Erick Gritch, a Lutheran scholar, and Roland Bainton of Yale, none of whom could have been accused of having an ecclesiastical axe to grind.

Flynn: And you wanted to show that those who call themselves conservatives are in reality revisionists?

Campbell: Yes! I'm a card-carrying member of the ACLU. I know who Isaac Backus and John Leland were. I know that they were Baptists of the colonies, and the First Amendment of the Constitution was their idea and that without them the notion of separation of Church and State, that the notion that is being so dangerously threatened by the revisionists, would not have been. And I know who Roger Williams was. The Baptist hijackers want Church and State to be one, and they are wrong. But, regrettably, they are prevailing.

Flynn: Were you able to do what you set out to do in *The Glad River*?

Campbell: Not really. My New York editor, a bright and skilled editor, said the Anabaptists might be the greatest thing since sliced bread, but she had never heard of them and they didn't belong in this novel.

Flynn: But don't you think you got the core of the story in what the main character, Doops Member, wrote in the jungle hospital?

Campbell: I tried, but I had to let Doops go crazy first.

Flynn: But don't you think the true Christian is always a little bit crazy? By the world's standards anyway?
Campbell: Uh huh.

Flynn: In the book, the prosecutor maintains that the character of Doops, Model T, and Kingston were all Communists. Did that bother you?
Campbell: Well, it was my story. The Anabaptists were not Communist. They were communitarians. They didn't build fortunes but shared what they had. That's right out of the New Testament. The radio and television preachers scream, "Money, money, money!" My three characters would never have sent them a dime. The Anabaptists believed that the death penalty was evil. Not the modern day electronic molesters. Certain Texas jurists would not have been permitted even to join the Anabaptist movement by reason of being jurists. They didn't believe in the death penalty [and] would not serve on juries or in the military.

Flynn: But you served in the military.
Campbell: More than that, I volunteered. I had a 4-D exemption. The replacement sergeant sent me to a hospital unit instead of an infantry division because his best friend was my uncle.

Flynn: So the scenes from Guadalcanal are from experiences serving in the hospital unit?
Campbell: Somewhat.

Flynn: One of the most powerful images in the book is that of a dying Japanese priest who was sitting in his own waste.
Campbell: I don't know where that came from. I think the novelist generally does not know where such scenes come from.

Flynn: The central character has a girl's name and is called "Doops," which does not seem very serious or important and he refuses to be baptized until he knows his name. How did he get his name?
Campbell: I was asked to write an article about a charismatic, snake-handling sect for a magazine. I have always been terrified by snakes, but for some reason I was not afraid as I sat a few feet from where the worshipers lifted up serpents, wrapped them around their necks, passed them from one to another. I was not afraid.

I was working on the novel at the time. So I let Doops attend such a service and he was not afraid. The normally unintelligible words somehow give him the clue of his name. And he is baptized by his friend, Model T, a Catholic, who is in jail for killing his young sweetheart.

Flynn: When Doops meets Kingston, the only member of the Neighborhood who doesn't get a name change, he tells Kingston that he is a neighbor but he will have to know him better to call him a friend. What's the difference?

Campbell: Buddies are like brothers, which is closer than friends. They call themselves the Neighborhood. Everyone is our neighbor. The Neighborhood is just the people who we love and trust the most. I've been told there is a small group of ministers, most of them in Texas, most of them Baptist, who call themselves the Neighborhood.

Flynn: Doops, who lives in Mississippi, says there are no Baptists left in the world. Do you know a Baptist Church?

Campbell: None of the big steeple outfits. I believe there is one in Nacogdoches. The pastor is Kyle Childress. Seventy-five members for fifteen years. That says something. I know of a church that has two lesbian pastors. I think that might be a Church. With a capitol C. The lesbian pastors don't make it a Church. The nonjudgmental parishioners do.

Flynn: What's your definition of a Church?

Campbell: My father was deacon in our little congregation in Mississippi. A fellow deacon got to messing around with a widow. He came before the deacon board, confessed his sin, and resigned his position as church treasurer. A motion was made, seconded, and passed to accept. He then stood and resigned his position as church organist. Motion. Seconded. Passed. Then he resigned as deacon and left the building. The young pastor, smelling blood and wanting to impress the deacon board, said that maybe they should go back to the old ways of discipline. Meaning the poor fellow would have to stand before the entire congregation, confess, and the congregation would then vote on whether or not to restore him to fellowship or turn him out completely.

After a period of awkward silence one of the younger deacons said to my father, "Uncle Lee, you're the senior deacon. What are you thinking?" Whereupon my father replied, "Well, if'n you hadn'a asked Uncle Lee what he was thinking, Uncle Lee wouldn't have told you. But since you asked,

Uncle Lee's a thinking, who's a gonna make the motion? And who's a gonna second it?" The meeting was adjourned because every deacon there, except Uncle Lee, had either been divorced or was married to a divorced woman. It was a good sermon on John 8:7.

Flynn: Then what is Communion?
Campbell: I was asked to speak to a national assembly of a denomination that has communion at every service. When asked, I told them that I had no feeling on how often they observed Communion. But I did remind them that during the time it took to celebrate the wafer and the cup, one thousand human beings would die of starvation and dehydration. Then I told them about a neighbor couple. The wife is on the vestry and he sees as his reasonable service cleaning the parking lot during the service. One this occasion, dressed in his outdoor work clothes he was almost finished when he saw a little piece of brownie. As he picked it up a street person saw him and thinking my friend was a fellow homeless person moved to him. "Hey, man. Don't eat that. Here eat this." He handed him a paper bag containing a fast food hamburger and a small Coca-Cola: No doubt it was his entire morning's work. Beggars don't make very much. That, I said, is the Sacrament of Communion.

Flynn: What are you working on now?
Campbell: I'm working on a pamphlet about Emmett Till. This is the fiftieth anniversary of his lynching. He started the civil rights movement.

Flynn: One of the Anabaptists in your novel says, "Writing can be idolatry."
Campbell: Well, it can be, can't it? Preaching is even worse, come to think about it.

Interview with Will Campbell

Tom Royals and Robert Evans / 2009

Interview conducted December 9, 2009, in Mount Juliet, Tennessee. Previously unpublished. Printed with permission.

Tom Royals: Will, you know Judge Evans and me. Bob is a circuit judge in Smith, Covington, Jasper, and Simpson counties. He went to the University of Mississippi for undergraduate and law school. I went to Millsaps and the University of Mississippi, in that order. I am a lawyer. We are having a conversation with you, similar to an interview or oral history. As you know, we are in your cabin behind your home in Mount Juliet, Tennessee. Thank you for giving us this opportunity.

Will Campbell: You went to Ole Miss Law School?

Bob Evans: I did. I went to both undergraduate and law school.

Will: Who was the dean when you were there?

Bob: Parham Williams.

Will: Oh, Parham was there?

Bob: Yes sir.

Will: He was a student when I was there.

Bob: That and he taught evidence. He was a tough teacher.

Will: He and his wife, Polly, were there. They are probably retired by now.

Bob: Really, I didn't know what ever became of him.

Tom: The dean helps law schools get accreditation. He was at Chapman, Sanford, and maybe Lincoln Memorial University, Duncan School of Law.

Tom: How may we address you?

Will: My name is Will.

Tom: How do you feel about being called Brother Will?

Will: I don't mind it—I don't insist on any title at all. I never liked Reverend.

Tom: What about Brother Will? Isn't there more than one meaning to that?

Will: Yes, but it's usually the same as—Brother Will.

Tom: Tell us about the Brotherhood: people who've ridden Tom T. Hall's bus?

Will: Yeah, well, usually we just named ourselves that. We traveled around on Tom's bus and did free shows. You were one of the brothers, weren't you?

Tom: Yes. Who all belonged? It would be Tom T. of course.

Will: It would have been Tom T., you, Jim Whitehead, Miller Williams, John Edgerton, and Alex Haley.

Tom: I understood Brotherhood at first required being published.

Will: No, not really—it helped to get us in.

Tom: What about nomination by another brother?

Will: Yes.

Tom: I remember you talked about the rules when you were speaking at St. Andrew's. You must have been walking out of there with another doctorate degree.

Bob: I've never heard the rules but I wondered if there were any.

Will: What did I say on that occasion?

Tom: I believe you said that it was an organization which is not really organized.

Will: Yeah.

Tom: And that it had some rules but nobody knew what they were.

Will: And that you had to do certain things but nobody knew what.

Tom: But it helped to have ridden on Tom T.'s bus.

Will: Yeah, that sounds right.

Tom: And then you said, "Like Tom Royals—he's a brother"—so I think that's how I got to be a brother. I had ridden on the bus. And you announced it.

Will: Yes.

Tom: Let's talk about some of the books you've written. *Race and Renewal of the Church* back in 1962.

Will: That's the first book I wrote.

Tom: What was going on when you wrote that book?

Will: Well, the Presbyterian publishing house, Westminster Press, was doing a series and they asked me to write anything I wanted to write about race relations. So that was kind of what I was doing at the time and nobody knew what I was doing. Nobody knew exactly what was going on in the South. I came back south from New York and did whatever I wanted to. If Little Rock broke out, I'd go to Little Rock. I spent the better part of the year in Little Rock. I went to New Orleans. I stayed out of Mississippi because I was in more danger in Mississippi than anywhere else.

Tom: Were there threats on your life?

Will: Yeah, and my family. I didn't want to put my parents in danger.

Bob: Was that about the same time that somebody tried to de-ordain you?

Will: That was a little earlier.

Tom: May we talk about it now?

Will: I was going by my full name, Will Davis, at that time and word got around that I had been ordained

Tom: Will Davis?

Will: Will Davis. I talked about this in my book about Joe, *Brother to a Dragonfly*. A man ought to be called what he wants to be called. If you want to be called Dave, we'll call you Dave.

Tom: When someone asks where you were educated, you tell them East Fork Consolidated High School. But Brother Will, didn't you go to some other schools? [Laughter]

Will: Well, of course, I went to school at East Fork Consolidated High School, and there were about a hundred kids from primer to twelfth grade all in one building, and that's where I went.

Tom: What county or town was that?

Will: There was no town. Liberty was the county seat. When people asked my daddy where we were from, he would say, "We get our mail at Liberty, we sell our cotton and shop in McComb. We live in the country."

Tom: Tell us about your family.

Will: Had one sister and two brothers. There were three boys and one girl. And we all went to East Fork Consolidated High School. And we had the primer back in those days—I don't think they have it now. I started first grade.

Tom: What did your brothers and sister goes on to do, as they say?

Will: Joe, the oldest boy and my mentor—

Tom: You've written about Joe in *Brother to a Dragonfly*?

Will: Yeah, he was a pharmacist. There were two stores in East Fork, a building and East Fork Baptist Church. And that was it. A man practiced medicine there in the building. When he stopped his practice, he left big black bottles in the building. Joe and I, Joe particularly, were enthralled by those big black bottles. We didn't know what they were but some kind of elixir, some kind of medicine. Dr. Stubblefield was his name as I recall. He left there, or died, or moved on or whatever. Then Joe went to the CCC Camp. Daddy had always insisted that all of his kids learn to type. I'm still grateful for his insight on that.

Tom: Do you think that helped you be a writer?

Will: No question about it. Daddy said if you know how to type you will always have a job. So Joe was the company clerk right out of high school. These were all country boys and he was the only one who knew how to type so they made him the company clerk. He decided to go to pharmacy school and Ole Miss didn't have a pharmacy school at that time. The nearest one was in Birmingham, at the college there. Howard College. Joe went to Howard College—of course Joe was the storyteller.

Tom: Was he a good storyteller?

Will: Oh, absolutely. He could tell about going to Howard College. He would say there's another Howard College but I was the wrong color so I went to Howard College for boys.

Tom: How much older was Joe than you, Brother Will?

Will: About eighteen months.

Tom: Was he the leader?

Will: Oh, by all means.

Tom: In later years it turned out that you—

Will: I became the leader.

Tom: We're going to get back to that story. Your family in south Mississippi was not rich, is that correct?

Will: That's right.

Tom: How would you describe their economic situation?

Will: My family?

Tom: Yes.

Will: Daddy always said that we were poor, but we're not trash. He would always make that distinction.

Tom: Was your Dad a reader?

Will: Not an avid reader but he, you know, when it got to the point he could—he subscribed to the *Jackson Daily News* which was about as bad a newspaper as you could get at that time.

Tom: So we know about Joe from *Brother to a Dragonfly*. He unfortunately had a dependence on pharmaceutical amphetamines and alcohol until his death.

Will: Yes.

Tom: Is that still painful for you to discuss, Will?

Will: Yes.

Tom: What did your sister do, Will?

Will: The sister didn't go to college. She graduated from high school and was courting this guy who went to Magnolia High School, played football— and his name was O. B. Honea.

Tom: Where is she—is she alive now?

Will: Sister?

Tom: Is your sister alive?

Will: No, sister died, uh, actually she died the same day that my Arkansas buddy died.

Tom: Is that right? I'm sorry, Brother Will.

Will: Yeah.

Tom: The same day Jim Whitehead died?

Will: And that is why I didn't go to Jim's funeral.

Tom: I didn't know that, Will. Bob and I were at Jim's funeral and expected to see you since we didn't know about your sister.

Will: Because I was at East Fork at my sister's funeral. I preached the funeral for my sister.

Tom: Brother Will, how did you work yourself out of that bad economic situation?

Will: I was always going to be a preacher.

Tom: At what age did you decide that?

Will: It my early teens.

Tom: Did you know the kind of preacher you were going to be?

Will: Yeah, well, the only preaching I knew was at East Fork Baptist Church. I'd never been to a Methodist or Presbyterian Church. Everybody was Baptist. Aunt Susie, my daddy's sister always called me the little preacher. When I was about four years old or younger, she sat me up on the pew at East Fork Church and I recited the 23rd Psalm. She started saying, "This is my little preacher." I didn't really make a decision. Aunt Susie said I was the little preacher.

Tom: When you were the little preacher did you think about the Old Testament versus the New Testament?

Will: No, it was a matter of believing in Jesus.

Tom: Were you taught to believe in Jesus based on faith alone?

Will: Right.

Tom: When did you first think of getting out of West Fork?

Will: Well, when I graduated from high school, there were eleven of us in my class.

Tom: Were you the most handsome?

Will: No.

Tom: I'll bet you were.

Bob: Why did you even have to ask such a question, Tom?

Will: Yes.

Bob: It's so obvious.

Tom: What influenced you the most as you pursued a Baptist pulpit?

Will: My senior class was at the church, which was next door to the school house, practicing for commencement. I had a big black hat which I put on and stepped up into the pulpit and stood up. The other students laughed. I said, "Why don't we have a youth day at East Fork Baptist Church?"

We chose Eve Lee, who I thought was my girlfriend, to play the piano. We had no organ. I would be the preacher, of course. And Delton would be the Sunday school superintendent and so on until all eleven of us had a part in the youth day at East Fork Baptist Church.

Tom: Who did the sermon?

Will: I wrote the sermon. I taped it on the cross piece of this seven-inch Oliver turning plow. I plowed and studied my sermon. Daddy told me if I didn't plow another row not to mess up in the church. You're the preacher that day and we are proud. I knew I had to go to college to be a preacher.

Tom: Is that what made you decide to go to college? You knew you had to get an education to be a preacher?

Will: Yes. After I preached that sermon at East Fork Baptist Church, I was invited to preach at East McComb Baptist Church. There was a fellow at church who had grown up there in the community and who then worked for Standard Oil in Baton Rouge. He came to our house that Sunday afternoon. I remember very well sitting on the front porch with my dad and the man. He asked me where I was going to college. My dad told him Southwest, a junior college in Summit.

Tom: What about LSU?

Will: The visitor pushed for Louisiana College but I thought he meant LSU and he actually drove me there and enrolled me. But I thought we were going to LSU. That's how I got to Louisiana College in Pineville, Louisiana.

Tom: So your father had a big influence on your education?

Will: Oh yeah, definitely so. I went for a year and a half, almost two years and then World War II began. I was already ordained and exempt. I thought if I went into the military, I would be where Joe was. So I joined. But I never saw Joe the three and one half years I was in the war. He was in Panama, and I was in the South Pacific.

Tom: How did you get into the army?

Will: I tried to volunteer for the navy and these big jocks just laughed at me. You know, I weighed about one hundred pounds and I didn't weigh enough to get in the navy, but I could get in the army. So I joined and went to basic training.

Tom: Why did you volunteer for the military?

Will: Just the romance of it and because Joe was in.

Bob: Was this right after Pearl Harbor?

Will: Yeah, well, yeah, I was a freshman at Louisiana College when Pearl Harbor happened. And I came back one Sunday afternoon from preaching down in Leesville, Louisiana, and heard about Pearl Harbor.

Tom: Were there debates about the justness of the war?

Will: No, no.

Tom: What was the attitude toward the war?

Will: It was our war. It wasn't that they had *attacked* us; we were going to whip them. And this Gordon Dorway and the other Cajun boy were mocking the Japanese army. Nobody said damn but that's what they meant. The Cajuns were saying the Japanese had only a few little planes. We would blow that island to kingdom come and it would soon be over.

Tom: What did you think?

Will: It sounded great to me. Count me in. I was ready.

Bob: Did the war bring attention to your religious beliefs?

Will: Yes.

Tom: Was Jesus the same as when you were a little boy?

Will: Yes, he was Jesus.

Tom: Jesus is Jesus?

Will: And I was Aunt Susie's little preacher.

Tom Did you ever feel yourself evolving, as Bob said?

Will: After the war I didn't go back to Louisiana College. I had met Brenda right in college. We wrote letters every day for the two and a half to three years I was in the army.

Tom: Where are those letters? Did she keep them?

Will: Yes, she kept them and I know where they are but they won't be used in an interview.

Bob: Come on, Will. You aren't going to tell us!

Tom: You're not going to try to put them in this interview. . . .

Bob: Let me ask you this. Did your war experience make you question religion?

Will: Well, yes it did in that we had people of different beliefs there. My best friend was a Jewish boy. And I didn't know what a Jew was. He was from Chicago.

Bob: He's the fellow who did the KP duty for you on Christmas?

Will: Yes, exactly. And he sent our picture home and his mother wrote back and said your buddy looks, like, I'm sure he's a nice boy but he looks goyish. I didn't know what the hell *goyish* meant. And I asked my buddy, what does that mean. He said "me and you, you goy. I'm Jew, you're goy."

Tom: You went from racial innocence to tough questions?

Will: I was in charge of a ward. I had to get the linens laundered every day. We had black and white patients. This black guy said, "You pick me out every time to get the dirty linens. Why is that?" Well I just, you know, we're soldiers and I'm in charge. I didn't have a reason. I told him that was his job. Our chaplain had gone to Union Seminary in New York. He talked to me openly about racism.

I went to Wake Forest because there were a number of North Carolina boys in my 107th Station Hospital unit there. And they would say, "We have a Baptist college in North Carolina, Wake Forest, and it's great—come up there. We'll get together every weekend, you know, and have a beer." I didn't see a one of those boys the three years I went to Wake Forest, not one time. After I was out of school, I was going through North Carolina when I remembered one of them named Donaby. I called him and he was very cold. He barely remembered me. Well, that was a long time ago.

Tom: That's just human nature, I guess.

Will: I thought if you were going to be the little preacher you would go to New Orleans Seminary after Louisiana College. Or if you were a pretty good student you'd go to the Louisville Baptist Seminary. I decided I wasn't going to do what I was supposed to do. By then I had kind of broken loose. I applied to Yale and didn't get in. How dare them.

Tom: Had they lost their minds?

Will: I was a little preacher and they were supposed to train little preachers. So I went to Tulane for a year and reapplied. I had figured out how to talk about labor relations management instead of Jesus. I took a course at Tulane in labor law and got a recommendation to Yale Divinity School. They accepted me just like that.

Tom: They were no match for you. And you got right in there?

Will: Yes.

Tom: Were you scheduled for combat in the war?

Will: Yes, all of us going in at that time were facing combat. A soldier from Coushatta, Louisiana, who knew my Uncle Clifton, put me in the medics. And that was a big turning point. In the infantry, they were all, well, trash, like I was.

Tom: That may be overstated. Were you disappointed not to get in the infantry?

Will: Oh, by all means, yes. Yes, I argued with the master sergeant who picked me out to go to the 107th Station Hospital.

Tom: What did he say?

Will: Well, he just looked at me and finally said, soldier, you don't know what the hell you're talking about.

Tom: Yes, you don't know what the hell you're talking about when you say you want to go to the infantry? Is that right?

Will: Yes. You know, I was known as a preacher though I wasn't a chaplain. But the other guys would refer to me, somewhat as preacher boy.

Tom: Well, how about Yale. How did they influence you?

Will: Well, the main reason I went there was the dean, whose name was Liston Polk, so by then my major interest was not so much race as labor, labor management. He had written this book which I had read called *Mill Hands and Preachers* about the famous Gastonia, North Carolina, strike. So that's why I went there and there was only one black student in my class so it was not a mixture.

Tom: Had you married Miss Brenda by then?

Will: Oh, yeah. I married her in January after I got out of the army in December.

Tom: Well, if you and Mrs. Brenda ever decide to release those love letters, I believe I can find a publisher quickly.

Will: I don't think that's going to happen, I don't know, but we wrote one another every day.

Tom: Yeah, that would be a great history of what happened during that period. What was big on civil rights about that time?

Will: Well, that decision was sort of made for us all. I remember the southern boys kind of hung together, you know. In fact, the dean, Liston Polk who had written the book about the Gastonia strike, one of his jokes was that the New England mothers all want to send their boys to Yale Divinity School to learn a southern accent. The majority of us were from the South, southern colleges.

Tom: Where did you go after Yale?

Will: I went to Taylor, Louisiana. All I wanted was to come back south. I didn't have any great desire to be a faithful Baptist by then. My best buddy then was a Methodist boy from Texas who was an Episcopalian. Back then at Yale we studied the prayer book and chose a denominational route. I took the Methodist route and went down to New York.

As a courtesy to annual conferences back home, we took a little exam and then we were supposed to march in and sit down on the front row in this church in New York and the bishop would come out and put his hand on our head and preach the sermon. He declared us as deacons or elders in the Methodist system and I would be a Methodist deacon.

Tom: Did you ever get declared to be a Methodist?

Will: No, that's what I'm leading up to.

Tom: Oh, I'm sorry, go ahead.

Will: There were, I think a dozen of us and we were marching in and the teacher said the last one in close the door and stay inside. Well, I was the last one in, but I closed it to the inside and I got on a train and went back to New Haven.

Tom: Wow.

Will: By then, I had gotten a call from a church in Louisiana, just interest. I wasn't positive that I wanted to be a Methodist preacher. There is something about being a Baptist; it's a disease. I closed the door to being a Methodist and got on a train. That's the only time in my life I ever had to see a psychiatrist. I went to Yale Methodist clinic and talked to this psychiatrist, Jewish I think. He was a pro who asked all the right questions. He said he could see just from just listening to me talk that I had made the sanest decision. So I said the hell with being a Methodist. I called this church in Louisiana and agreed to a trial sermon. After the trial sermon they called me. I graduated from Yale Divinity School, went to Taylor, Louisiana, in Bienville Parish, and all of a sudden I was a Baptist preacher.

Tom: Did you have any questions about the Baptist dogma?

Will: I probably wasn't quite sure I wanted to be a preacher of any kind by then, because my major interest was the boys from the South at Yale Divinity School. After the Supreme Court decision outlawing racial segregation in public schools, we would get together and lament the fact that here we had gone to Yale to go back south and integrate. What the hell are we supposed to do now? You know. Well, I was interested in this little village because I was also interested in labor management relations. This was a saw mill town and that got me in trouble right away. There was a paper mill strike in Elizabeth, Louisiana. The owner of that paper mill was from Florida and he couldn't even come over and negotiate on weekends because he was a Baptist and he had to go to church. He was a deacon in the Baptist Church, somewhere in Florida. And that struck me. Something is not right about this. The race issue was not over.

Tom: You thought *Brown v. Board* had settled that issue?

Will: Yeah, but I knew that race relations were still to go, and I was going to work in race and labor management. That wasn't over either.

Tom: So what was your next career move?

Will: At Yale I had chosen labor. So I went down to Elizabeth, Louisiana, and spoke to labor unions that were on strike and it's a wonder I wasn't killed. There was a guy, I learned later, who was chosen to kill that Yankee preacher but he died of an accident the night before I was to speak down there. I had a little sophistication by then and discounted many things.

Tom: In spite of the setbacks, did you still feel that God had a definite place for you?

Will: Yes, but I wasn't quite sure what it was.

Tom: Are Jesus and God two different things? How does that work?

Will: Well, no, it's not the same thing. Jesus, in my understanding of the New Testament, was God, the Father, Son, and Holy Ghost. You know I believed that and still do, but maybe not as strongly.

Tom: Do we have more than one God?

Will: Yes, that's about what it works out to be.

Tom: Have you read the Jesus scholar writings?

Bob: Crossan.

Tom: Crossan, Dominic Crossan and those guys who call themselves the Jesus Seminar?

Will: I went to school with some of them.

Tom: Would you talk a minute about the pre-Easter Jesus and the post-Easter Jesus.

Will: I wouldn't be an authority on that—I never took it too seriously one way or the other. I don't know—there is so much about scripture that I don't know or understand.

Bob: Merrill Hawkins, in his book about you, said you seemed to make no distinction between fundamentalist departures from authentic religion and modern educated urbane departures. What's he talking about?

Will: I don't know—I'll see him next week.

Bob: Do ask him—I want to know what those departures are.

Will: I never read that book but I remember he's now teaching at the school where I'm getting an honorary degree—

Bob: He was at Mercer at one point wasn't he?

Will: Yeah, he wasn't on the faculty.

Bob: When I read that I thought, okay, what is authentic religion in Will Campbell's mind and how did the fundamentalist depart and the urbane depart from the authentic religion?

Will: I don't know.

Bob: Authentic as started by Jesus I assume. I'm thinking authentic religion is, and Will may agree, simply, love your neighbors and your enemies, and free the prisoners.

Will: Yes, right.

Bob: That's pretty damn hard.

Will: Gets tough along there somewhere.

Bob: Is that part of authentic religion?

Will: Sure, I think it is. That's why I got into labor management relations and that's why I got in to race relation.

Bob: Which is an attempted application of those principles, I guess.

Will: There is something wrong with any Jesus who thought whites were better than darker people. It didn't make any sense to me.

Tom: Do you see any evidence that Jesus ever got into problems between the races? The historical Jesus, I guess I'm talking about, Jesus who lived, preached.

Will: Well there was no such thing at the time and Jesus would not have known race relations—there weren't any.

Tom: But he knew economic divisions though?

Will: Yeah, sure, the people he ran with and he picked you know, as my daddy would say, and his daddy before him; they weren't theological scholars but they knew something about the Bible and that's what they were thinking about. When Jesus picked some good ole boys, he picked his own kind of people.

Tom: To help him carry the message?

Will: Yes.

Tom: National Council of Churches: not everybody joined?

Will: Not all of them. Southern Baptist never joined.

Bob: They don't believe much in ecumenical enterprises.

Tom: At one point you were connected to them?

Will: I worked for them. That's how I got out of Mississippi. They appropriated money to put me in charge of integrating the South. And I chose to work from Nashville.

Tom: Integrating the South? By yourself?

Will: That is right.

Bob: I guess your to-do list was pretty long, wasn't it?

Tom: I'm looking here at Merrill M. Hawkins Jr.'s book *Will Campbell: Radical Prophet of the South.*

Will: Yeah, that was his PhD dissertation at Baylor. I didn't know him. He teaches at Carson-Newman College in Tennessee now.

Tom: He avers that your departure from the National Council of Churches marked the end of any traditional ministry for you. Do you agree?

Will: No, not really. No, you know I do the same thing I've always done, help the widows, orphans, especially the widows.

Tom: Although Hawkins did add that you, Will Campbell, considered yourself to be a preacher.

Will: I never read that book.

Tom: He treated you well. He separated the work of the preacher from employment by institutional religion—what is institutional religion here?

Will: Steeples.

Tom: Steeples? Okay.

Will: First Baptist, United Methodist, and whatever you have—y'all got a woman bishop down there, don't you?

Bob: I believe the Methodists do. In fact, the Methodist church there in the little town of Raleigh, they hired a female pastor and I was curious as to how the locals would respond. They fell in love with her and she did a remarkable job. You know the Methodists swap out every couple of years—they hated to see her go. I did too. She did wonderful sermons.

Will: They generally do—they have to.

Bob: And a friend of mine who is single was going to the Baptist church across the street, but when Mary came, he felt the Lord calling him to become a Methodist over there.

Will: No question—the Lord will do that. Call you where the pretty pastor is.

Tom: Brother Will, when a minister says he has been called to go somewhere—

Will: He's lying. The Lord always calls where the pay is a little more.

Tom: I wonder why they feel it necessary to say they have been called rather than "I just got a better deal."

Will: They're hypocrites.

Tom: Like I was arguing in court the day before yesterday.

Bob: What was that trial over there about?

Tom: It was a drug case—they had stopped the guy and said they got permission to search. I was arguing they shouldn't have searched the van because they arrested him and he was not free to go and they didn't have a right to get permission from him. But they say, of course, that he would have been free to go at any time.

Will: Of course.

Tom: There may be many kinds of legal lies. "He was free to go" being a major one. You could argue Jesus was free to go if he hadn't been so stubborn.

Will: Yeah, right—that's a big one.

Tom: And so on—such as, I feel sympathy for the poor and many of those others. Do you think of any legal lies?

Bob: Legal lies?

Tom: That's how I just referred to them.

Bob: I just came through eight years of them. It shouldn't be hard to scrape up a few.

Tom: Would you think most any kind of lying would finally be harmful some way?

Will: I don't know—I'm not in charge of the punishment—I don't believe in punishment really.

Tom: I don't mean punishing people for telling lies. I mean, how much harm do lies do to the structure in the village?

Will: It doesn't really hurt.

Tom: Doesn't hurt a lot, we just get used to it and accept it, like political lies—he's going to clean up the country or whatever or clean up gambling. Of course they know they can't clean up gambling and prostitution.

Will: In Amite County they were going to clean up the bootleggers, and the bootlegger invariably paid the sheriff and they went right on making the shine. Van Causey was the sheriff when I was a kid and everybody knew that the local bootleggers gave him more money every month than his legal salary.

Tom: Didn't bother them. Well, these lies get so comfortable, it makes me nervous every now and then. But like you say it's part of the way we do. Do you remember discussing that with Merrill Hawkins?

Will: I barely remember meeting him.

Tom: Well, he wrote a pretty good book about you.

Bob: You ought to read it—you might learn something.

Will: Yes, he and his wife sat right over there and spent about three or four hours with me and went home and wrote his—he had his PhD dissertation at Baylor.

Tom: And he put a great picture on the front of the book. You owe him.

Bob: Who is that fellow—good-looking young man?

Will: Nice-looking hat.

Tom: Good-looking glasses, intelligent-looking fellow.

Will: That must be a picture that Al Clayton made. Al is a professional photographer, or was.

Bob: You did a book with him—*Covenant.*

Will: *Covenant,* right.

Bob: I've got that book—it's a good book

Will: You know more about my books than I do.

Bob: I've read them, you just wrote them—that's all you did.

Will: I never read them.

Bob: Somebody asked me something about a book I did once and I said I didn't read it, I just wrote it. I recommend your books to you.

Tom: You need to read this one by Hawkins—you'd learn a lot of good stuff about yourself.

Will: I will see him next week.

Tom: He talks about "out from under the steeples" and about ethics and theology. Is he saying you did theology when you were under the steeples and relied on ethics when you got out?

Will: I guess—that's PhD talk.

Tom: Now, he quoted Cecelia from *Cecelia's Sin* and from *Glad River* on the truth of the non-institutional church as you teach it: where a few of the faithful are gathered there is a church.

Will: I will say that, I believe it.

Bob: You mentioned just in passing that someone might refuse to recognize one of your baptisms.

Tom: Were you talking about my baptism?

Will: Yeah that was it—Dean Edwin Bacon, dean at St. Andrew's Cathedral in Jackson.

Bob: What did he have to say about that?

Will: Well, Dean Bacon might have mentioned immersion since he was Baptist at one time. However, since he became an Episcopalian he would have no problem with that. I told counsel here to tell the dean that we had done it in Latin. Tom, do you still have that I hope.

Tom: Yes, I do. I took it to Dean Bacon and he got a good laugh out of it being in Latin. Of course he accepted it and never intended not to, but you made your point.

Will: Yes, he went to Mercer.

Tom: And he was one of the good people over there?

Will: Yes, absolutely. He is now the dean at All Saints Episcopal Church in Pasadena, one of the largest churches in California.

Tom: I was talking to Dean J. Edwin Bacon about joining St. Andrew's. He let me by on some issues but reacted strongly to my not having been baptized at age fifty. I would have had to march down on Easter morning with several newborn babies to be baptized by the dean. So I said I'll ask Brother Will to baptize me when I'm up there. He said well, alright, Brother Will is a fine man.

Will: Yeah I'll buy that—he better not argue with me. I know too much on him.

Bob: But there is not a better fellow to have baptized you than Will.

Will: Yeah, right.

Tom: And I was fortunate to have Brother Will baptize me.

Will: I've got a copy of the baptism I'll show you, Judge.

Bob: Yes, I'd love to see it.

Will: The Latin was written by a PhD in Latin, at Vanderbilt. She is a great friend.

Bob: Along that line, some say *Providence* was your. most literary book, partly fiction?

Will: No, no, that's very much the way that happened.

Bob: As I recollect, you didn't think much of your neighbor Andrew Jackson.

Will: No.

Bob: His place isn't far from here I believe.

Tom: In fact, I remember you were pretty hard on ol' Andrew about the Indian issues.

Will: I imagine he used to own this spot where we are sitting.

Bob: Might have.

Will: He owned half of Tennessee.

Tom: Speaking of Mercer, what happened to Simi Oni?

Will: Oni, yeah, Sim Oni, an African. He was converted by Mercer and then Mercer wouldn't admit him as a student. So they finally did and that's when I met him and wrote a book about him. I don't know where Sim is now. He went back to Africa, and on the anniversary of his haven't been being admitted to Mercer, he came back and came by a couple of times needing money.

Tom: What made Mercer finally admit him?

Will: Well, it was a great embarrassment that a Mercer missionary converted Oni. And then the school denied their convert admission. We'll make him a Christian but we won't educate him. Some of us used that to our advantage or the Lord's advantage.

Tom: You and Edwin Bacon must have had a field day.

Will: Yeah—what's the name of the book I wrote about Duncan Gray?

Bob: *And Also with You: Duncan Gray and the American Dilemma.*

Will: You know more about my work than I do.

Bob: I'm saying you ought to read it.

Will: I've heard it's a pretty good book.

Bob: It is a pretty good book. You got some kind of award as I recollect.

Tom: I like *Glad River.* The Anabaptists character, Doops, is one of my favorite characters.

Will: Doops Bombar. That was *Glad River.*

Tom: How did that book come about?

Will: Well, that was purely fiction. That is the yarn I made up. There are people who say that everything Campbell ever wrote was made up. Some of it I wish I had, like *Brother to a Dragonfly.* I wish I had made that up, but I didn't—that's the way that happened.

Tom: I believe I'd recommend *Dragonfly*, *Forty Acres and a Goat*, *Providence*, and *Glad River* to anyone who hasn't read them, if there is anyone like that, except you, Will.

Bob: I'll tell you one I really liked. Please comment on *Convention*.

Will: Yeah, I liked it too. You being a Baptist, you knew what I was talking about.

Bob: I wish some folks in Nashville would read it.

Will: They don't like Campbell in Nashville.

Tom: Benjamin Houston did a good interview with Will on civil rights in Nashville in 2003.

Bob: Yes, I saw that.

Tom: You reckon we'd better get the health care program through?

Will: Some kind. I don't think it will be what Obama wished for—could be something I think.

Bob: You never get all you want in legislation.

Tom: What do you think about Obama winning the Nobel Peace Prize?

Will: That's their business, a little unusual I thought, but that's their prize. They can give it to anyone they want to.

Bob: In fact, he gave his speech this morning, I believe, the acceptance speech. I just saw a clip from the news, and in paraphrasing he said "Sometimes war is necessary." How do you feel about that remark?

Will: I don't like it.

Bob: He said wars are necessary when nations like Iran and North Korea are playing with nuclear weapons and we cannot close our eyes to it—I believe his words were.

Will: Well, that's true but what is he going to do about it? I don't know, particularly, since we started the nuclear weapons.

Bob: We're responsible. I remember reading a little passage you wrote about being in the South Pacific, I think Saipan, when they dropped the bomb on Hiroshima. What was your response to that?

Will: Well, I was delighted. I was thinking about going home—seeing Brenda. I hadn't seen her in two and a half years. So, you know, I was in there with the rest of them.

Tom: Back to books; I would think another good place to start reading Will would be *Soul among Lions*, wouldn't you, Bob?

Bob: That's a great book.

Tom: In *Soul among Lions* you wrote about your favorite subjects, didn't you, Will?

Will: Yes.

Bob: Wasn't that on a TV?

Will: Yeah—the Methodists had a TV show. I forgot what they called it and I was one of four. I think one guy hated me. I think he was a Methodist preacher around Detroit or somewhere and wasn't worth a damn; of course, he thought I wasn't either.

Tom: What was the roughest part of the civil rights movement for you?

Will: I don't know—it was all dangerous. I was in more danger because I was a turncoat. I wasn't raised that way and Yankees came down here and interfered. They didn't know anything but I knew better. I was raised in Amite County, Mississippi, from the roughest state in the Union and I guess Amite County is considered the roughest, if not one of the roughest counties in the State of Mississippi. When you are that age, I guess, you think, well hell, they won't kill me. I'm not born to die. Doing the Lord's work, or whatever I'm doing, they're not going to kill me.

Bob: How did that make you feel, emotionally, that your lifelong friends and, I imagine, some of your family hated you and considered you a turncoat?

Will: Well, you know, a mixed bag, I suppose—but I was so convinced that, to coin a phrase, I was called to do what I was doing and so if they were going to kill me then they gotta answer for that. I would answer to it if I failed to do what I was born to do.

Bob: There still must have been some personal hurt in it.

Will: Sure—but now they were in the East Fork community and East Fork Baptist Church and we'd all gone to school together and most of us were cousins. Now they were having the two hundredth anniversary of East Fork Baptist Church. They asked me to come and be one of the speakers. I didn't know whether Brenda would be up to it. But was that a cop out? I saw back to the picture which was at the end of my senior year in high school. I was seventeen years old. Grandpa stood above me. I remember it so well. I was kneeling down there and he had his hand pressed on my head. He was tough but tears were falling. He wasn't tough in the sense of drinking or gambling or nothing like that but he was tough.

Bob: A hard life will toughen you up.

Will: And he was literally weeping—I was the only Campbell who had made a preacher. Though I was going to Louisiana College the next month to study to be a preacher, I was already a preacher. I had given my first sermon at this church: East Fork Baptist Church.

Tom: So you would still be a Baptist today, right?

Will: Right

Tom: A Baptist minister?

Will: Yeah.

Bob: You got papers?

Will: Yeah—there's no way to quit. How do you just quit?

Bob: You can't just say "take your ordination book back"? It doesn't work like that?

Will: No.

Tom: Did you speak at the church?

Will: Yes, a couple of guys came to the rescue. They weren't church people anymore. They sent word. "If you try to take Will Davis apart and take the ordination away from him, we'll come down there and filibuster that church to the ground."

Bob: Friends like that are rare.

Will: And that was that. Even they were afraid to commit a cardinal sin by disrupting the church. They had rather just let me be a preacher. Some people still know how that church was started over at Chandler's Bridge on the East Fork of the Amite River.

Tom: Will, let's switch to your prison ministry.

Will: That is a family thing through Grandpa and my daddy. I was telling you yesterday about Grandpa taking his boys on a fifteen-mile wagon ride to Liberty to see Allen Westbrook hanged.

Tom: Was that a black person?

Will: No, he was white. And my mother and her sister had heard the crime committed. I can take you right to the spot where Allen Westbrook shot his father-in-law and mother-in-law dead and then tried he get a ride to Liberty and went to the sheriff and turned himself in. He said, "I'm the murderer and I know you're going to lock me up. I've got to pay for my crime but they had it coming." It was his in-laws. My mother and Aunt Dolly, two little girls, were playing—I can take you right to the house where they were play-ing—and they heard this screaming and gunshot and heard the scream con-tinuing and heard another gunshot. The victims were both running when he shot them. Daddy remembered the speech he made. He said: "If I had listened to my mother I wouldn't be standing here today." His in-laws would gossip about him. They would say Westbrook was a drunk or whatever. His wife would tell him. He went in on them one day. I was going to buy the gun that was used for one hundred dollars, but Dad discouraged me.

Tom: I know a guy told me one time if you carry a gun, you might kill somebody with it. If you don't carry a gun, you won't kill anybody with it.

Will: Yeah, that's right.

Tom: Did you counsel with Sam Bowers?

Will: Counsel may not be the right word. But I did visit him in prison. The high sheriff, McMillin, said Bowers would want to talk politics so we had a long visit and I saw him later on occasions.

Tom: What was his status then? Was he charged or convicted?

Will: He was convicted.

Bob: Didn't you kind of do a little trip with him through the south part of Smith County one time?

Will: I sure did, yeah. I sure did.

Tom: Okay, I've got a specific question about that.

Will: We can ask the Judge that question.

Bob: I'm out of my jurisdiction up here. Where did y'all go? I know you went around Mize somewhere.

Will: Yeah, we started out at Mize at a store there. I don't know why I never liked Ken Dean. For some reason—he's a smart ass. But he—well there's something I ought not to say so I won't say it. That way I won't have to strike it out of your text draft.

Tom: Let's go to this trip you took with Sam Bowers. Gene Tullos, does that name ring a bell with you? Gene is a lawyer there in Smith County. He's a friend of mine and a friend of Judge Evans.

Will: Yeah, yeah, I met him one time—he lived in Laurel, didn't he?

Tom: He's the one that built a mansion in Smith County that copies one of the Natchez houses perfectly. He copied all the furniture also. He's a Civil War historian.

Will: Yeah, I met him but I didn't get to know him. But I think he was at Sam's trial in Hattiesburg.

Tom: He may have been—he had some interest in it. I was visiting with him the other day and I told him I was going to see you and he asked me to give you his regards and to ask you a specific question. He said that Sam was looking at someone's grave down there in Smith County.

Will: Smith County—that's a true story. I can tell you the story.

Bob: Okay, do that.

Will: Bowers started talking to the person in the grave. And he turned to us and Kenneth Dean was with him and he said something to the effect that this is not a matter of superstition. It is his spirit. We're very close and his spirit is still around. We communicate to that effect. And it was very moving, the tribute to his dead friend—he said, "He was my best friend."

Tom: He was in the grave?

Will: He said to the spirit, "If the spirit is in," and I don't know. I think he even said, I don't know, but "If you are still lingering and you hear me."

Bob: Do you remember the name?

Tom: Of who was in the grave?

Will: I don't remember—he called his name.

Tom: Was it Williams?

Will: I can't recall, seems like it was.

Tom: How would we find that out if we wanted to know?

Will: Well, I could call Ken Dean and he would tell me in a second.

Tom: Would you mind making a note to do that? We'd like to have that name and Gene is very interested in it. We would like to have the name in this interview if we can get it. Need something to write with?

Will: Yeah.

Tom: Now you didn't promise us you were going to do our research, did you?

Will: What?

Tom: You didn't promise us you would do any research for us, did you?

Bob: That's going to cost us extra.

Tom: Lord, I know it. Let's take a break. I'll call and ask him that name.

Will: Who?

Bob: Gene Tullos.

Tom: He was the one asking.

Bob: There's my note—I've got to pick me up a country ham before I go home.

Will: The best are right down the road.

Tom: God in heaven. What do I have to do to get you two to be serious?

Bob: What store—do you remember the name of the store?

Will: Yeah, I go past it every day. Well I'll just go with you.

Tom: We might want to go get a bite to eat here in a minute.

Will: We'll do that.

Bob: I'll get Gene on the phone while you're hunting the number. [Talking on phone to Gene Tullos's office—saying it's not urgent]

Will: Well, I'd expect they think we're not urgent.

Tom: I feel very urgent.

Bob: Curb your urgency. Just going after those hams is urgent.

Tom: Gene was thinking the story went that Bowers said as he teared up, "That's the best friend I ever had in my life."

Will: That's close enough.

Tom: While we're thinking—is there anything you could tell us about Bowers that is not confidential?

Will: Not really. I have right here some letters. I think I kept them. He would write me letters from prison—ten to fifteen pages of handwritten letters but it was mostly not anything—he never told me any of the secrets, not at all.

Tom: What other clan figures did you talk to? I don't mean they have to be named.

Will: Well, my cousins.

Tom: That was the family, the church?

Bob: What about Preacher Killen from down around Philadelphia—did you ever run across him—he's doing time now—he was convicted a year or so ago, a couple of years ago.

Will: Yeah, what was he convicted of?

Bob: Conspiracy and the murder of Goodwin, Schwerner, and Chaney.

Will: Yeah, that's right. Yeah, I was at one of those trials but I didn't know him really. I just knew who he was.

Tom: Did you go into the cell and talk to any of the condemned people who were on death row?

Will: On death row?

Tom: On death row, or any of the civil rights people who were convicted of civil rights violations?

Will: Not that I recall at the moment. But I never—I don't mean to sound pious here—but I never kept tabs on the charges. That wasn't my business really. I don't mean to sound too pious.

Tom: What called you there? That was obviously a calling of sorts to do that.

Will: Well, I mean, my God, the story of Jesus in the New Testament is filled with it. That was his main kick you know, visiting the prisoners.

Bob: Freedom, he said.

Will: Yes.

Bob: How would you comfort somebody in that situation? What could you tell them to make them feel better?

Will: I don't have any idea what I can do to help you, but I'm here and I'm your friend. That's all I need to tell you, I'm your friend. Of course, that narrowed it down because they had been through your courts.

Bob: Been through my system.

Will: And defense counsel, so you've done all you can do or should, I suppose.

Tom: By that time had most of them accepted the Lord in some way—had they counseled with somebody in prison already?

Will: A lot of them.

Tom: What did they want to pass on to you?

Will: You didn't have to come to see me.

Bob: Any of them ever say, "Get the hell away from me—leave me alone"?

Will: No, never had one turn me away.

Tom: Any of them ask you to pray with them?

Will: Yeah, oh yeah.

Tom: Did you baptize one of them in prison?

Will: Yeah, but I don't remember who it was now.

Tom: Well, how does the judge and the defense lawyer and the preacher deal with the admonition of Jesus to let the prisoners go? Surely Jesus was talking about political prisoners.

Will: How do you know?

Tom: I'm guessing.

Will: You are guessing.

Tom: Yes, I am guessing—do you think I'm wrong?

Will: Yes.

Tom: I'm glad you told me then.

Bob: He said free the prisoners and he didn't say legal or political but free the captives. Set the captives free. Causes me a little personal problem sometime because of the business I'm in.

Will: Yeah, of course, sure, yeah.

Tom: Yes, but was he talking about the Romans who—or was he—who had locked up Jews on political crimes—and I don't know that. And it's probably not true.

Will: I'm not the projected counsel here, but Jesus was talking to the judges. He wasn't talking to politicians.

Bob: Oh man, I hate to hear that. Of course, as a Baptist, I would say that he was talking about from the captivity of sin and that's a good weasel out.

Will: That's not what he said.

Tom: What about the idea that these Jews were living in a bubble in the Romans' society. The Romans had an empire to run. They had legions out—they had to raise taxes to protect the Romans and the Jews and they also were passing forward the wisdom of the Greeks and teaching languages—they had those responsibilities that the Jews didn't have. The Jews had the protection of the Romans, so they could say hit me again on the other side of the face, and they could talk in ways and feel ways and feel sympathy that the Romans could not feel. Do you see anything there?

Will: I don't know. Jesus was a strange cat.

Tom: Yes, he was.

Bob: He was radical.

Will: Yes, he was.

Bob: You and I had a discussion one time about the movement being still active. I suppose, these folks want old-time religion, and you said, "No, they don't." Why don't they?

Will: Well, it would be too radical for them. They don't really know what they are asking for.

Bob: They're asking for the captives to be set free and we love our enemies—that's hard to do.

Will: Yes, I know.

Bob: Yes, you know better than I, of course you do.

Will: Not really.

Tom: Did you spend any time with Martin Luther King?

Will: A lot.

Tom: Tell us everything you can and want to and would share about Martin Luther King.

Will: Oh God, the first time I met Martin, he was nobody. He'd just gone down to Ebenezer Baptist Church in Atlanta where he pastored with his daddy about 1960, and I was working in race relations at Ole Miss and the movement was going on and he was probably mentioned all the time. He was being tried on some minor thing and I went to the court where he was being tried. Of course, he was convicted, your colleagues killed—

Tom: Was this a municipal court on a misdemeanor for marching or something like that?

Will: Yes. And when we left, his church was just a block or so from the court, so there was a crowd out there and this one guy kept coming on the sidewalk and bumping Rev. King off the street into the crowd. Martin just got back on the sidewalk and kept walking. Finally Martin, looked him in his face and said "You know, I love you." The guy said, "You old—something— kiss my ass or something—I don't love you."
   Later I went to his secretary. I don't remember her name, but I remember what she looked like: beautiful. I told her I didn't want to bother Rev. King, but I'd like to speak, and shake his hand. So all of a sudden I saw this figure through the door and he said, "Hey brother, come on back here." So he came out, you know, and shook my hand and I said, "Well I was in the courtroom over there and I was walking down here and I saw this guy keep bumping into you and you told him you loved him. Do you love me?" He said, "Brother, come on in and sit down here." So that was the first time I ever talked to him and since then we have been dear friends. Of course, we had a lot to talk about. He had gone up to a Yankee school like I had, not the same one but might as well have been.
   Once when I saw him they were trying to take his PhD away from him. By then, Martin Luther King was famous, a world famous Rhodes Scholar and all that. But they were afraid of him naturally, and I understand that.

Tom: But he continued to keep the title?

Will: Oh yeah.

Bob: How did y'all come to form the Southern Christian Leadership Conference?

Will: Well, I didn't really have anything to do with that. I did in a sense. There was a meeting, there are so many documents that I haven't kept that I should have. I remember right there on that table for years and years there was a document calling to action or something like that. It went to black ministers in the South calling them to meet in Atlanta. I went but somebody's house, maybe Ralph Abernathy's, had been dynamited the night before. Martin and Ralph had to leave Atlanta and go back to Montgomery so they weren't at this first meeting. It was about transportation, protesting segregated buses. The guy running the meeting was the black teamster's president I think.

Anyway he worked with them and he was a very, very well-known radical. He said "Now, Rev. Campbell, we appreciate your being here but this, I want you to understand, is just for black pastors." But another official said look, before this thing is over we're going to need all the help we can get, black, white, purple, anything—so you let your brother in. So they said, "Okay. This guy that had worked with Martin down at Montgomery and was very well known." I went in and I was a young and foolish prophet. I volunteered to be of service. I would take the document they wrote and see that it was on the desk of every congressman in Washington by Monday morning. The presiding official said, "No, we can't. We appreciate our brother's help but we can't let him do that."

Bob: The document was about the Southern Christian Leadership Conference?

Will: Yeah, yeah, and that was the formation of it, actually, it was formed there, it was the following week in New Orleans where they had another meeting and I went to that. That's when it was named Southern Christian Leadership Conference.

Tom: How long did you remain friends with Martin Luther King?

Will: Until he died.

Tom: Were you in or near or around that tour he was on when he was shot?

Will: No, I had just come back. I could show you right at the door you came in this morning. I was out there chopping wood, I still heated the old house with wood, and Brenda came to the door. I had just come back from Memphis, had been back an hour or so. Brenda said, well, "Martin just got shot." And I said "He's dead." She said "They didn't say he was dead, they just said he was shot." I said, "Call the airport because he's dead."

So there was a flight back and as soon as I could get to the airport, I got to Memphis within an hour or two after his death and there were airplanes flying over Memphis and it was as dark as a dungeon. The whole city was blacked out. There were one or two cabs at the airport. I rented a motel, as I recall, I'm not positive. I got the only black driver. He took me to the Lorraine Motel. When I got there, that's where those pictures were made.

Tom: Yeah, I've got one of those pictures somewhere.

Will: I've got a good picture. I forgot who has it, of me standing on the balcony looking and I was by myself—I don't know who's got that picture. That's the best one.

Tom: You know, Will, Buddha would suggest, I think, that everybody go out and try to be a Buddha of some sort. Was Jesus suggesting that Christians go out and be Jesus-like, and be able to follow the "do unto others" rule?

Will: I doubt it. I don't know. I think it was simply saying be a good ole boy, you know, treating everybody like you want to be treated.

Tom: Of course, that was nothing new that had been said for thousands of years by others. Buddha had said that.

Bob: What about take up your cross and relax? Is that what is being preached to us today?

Will: Yeah, I think so—take up your cross and relax? It seems like I heard somebody say that.

Bob: You wrote it—and I could only guess the context.

Tom: Well, I guess Plato, maybe, could speak of the Jesus who would turn the other cheek and do these kinds of things.

Will: Don't you dread to see a Millsaps lawyer come into your court? They know everything.

Bob: What we don't tell them is they gave us extra information at Ole Miss about how to handle Millsaps lawyers. We got a special course in it. Sorry, counsel.

Tom: I know. How close—well I'm withdrawing the question. Have you ever known anybody who approached being Jesus-like? By Jesus-like, I mean what we've been talking about, turning the other cheek, doing unto your brother exactly what you wanted from him.

Will: Not really. I've know some who tried.

Tom: Did Dr. King mean it when he told the redneck guy [pushing him off the sidewalk] that he loved him?

Will: I don't know—I wonder some time how one could love him. He didn't know who the guy was.

Tom: And not just Martin, I mean, would anybody mean it?

Will: Yes.

Bob: You could say it in the abstract—I love my fellow man—but I don't like this one over here too much.

Will: SOB pushed me off the sidewalk.

Bob: Yes, pushed me off the sidewalk.

Tom: Were there any other well-known people in the civil rights movement that you were friends with or counseled with?

Will: Abernathy—I visited with him in the Memphis jail.

Tom: What was he charged with?

Will: Trespassing or something.

Tom: Yeah, okay, right. What do you think about Gandhi? Passive resistance?

Will: Well, I think he was on to something. He certainly influenced Martin and even more so Jim Lawson. And Lawson, Jim Lawson—I have mentioned him—was, I think, the only truly nonviolent person I ever knew. If I went into his residence and said I'm going to take your children or even say I'm going to hurt your children, I don't think he would have struck back. I think Martin would have.

Tom: Yes. Well, I guess somebody has to set that example. It's a far distance from here to any widespread deportment such as that, wouldn't you think?

Will: Of what?

Tom: Long time before we see a lot of people like Lawson?

Will: Yes.

Tom: Well, let's change gears here. Many of your fans want to hear about your celebrity followers. Such as the country musicians who came to you as their guru and as their oracle. What brought you together with them?

Will: Poverty, I think.

Tom: How is that?

Will: Whenever new people came into Nashville to seek their fortune, they lived on 16th Avenue, a more affordable location. That's where I lived, so we ran into each other.

Tom: Please go on.

Will: See, I didn't know Johnny [Cash] as well as I knew Waylon [Jennings] or Tom T. [Hall]. I'm not sure anybody did. A person told me, "Johnny said I was his closest friend." That person went on to say that if he were Johnny's closest friend, Johnny was hard up for friendship because this person barely knew him. Johnny was hard to know. You liked him, but you knew very little about him really.

Tom: Did you equate Johnny's problem with Joe's problem?

Will: Something like that. I have never articulated that even in my own mind but I did.

Tom: Maybe you had a soft spot for John because of that—do you think he fought the same kind of battle that your brother fought?

Will: Well, I think Joe's was a more personal thing.

Bob: You had the office downtown one time, is that right?

Will: Yeah.

Bob: Is that about when you first came here?

Will: Yeah.

Bob: And all kind of folks wandered in and out of there, I suppose.

Will: I finished this stupid book. A lot of things you are referring to here are in this book. Not about Johnny so much, I didn't know Johnny very well then, but Kristofferson.

Tom: Yeah, that's a good story—tell us about Kris.

Will: Let's stop the tape a minute and let me find that—yeah, okay.

Tom: Okay, while you looked, we were talking about that guy who was Bowers's friend in the grave.

Will: Sam Bowers.

Tom: Bob called the lawyer, Gene Tullos. He called back during lunch and the guy's name was what, Judge?

Bob: Billy Sullivan.

Will: Is that his name?

Bob: That's what Gene said it was.

Will: That sounds right. But, of course, Bowers, they all had pet names and he probably didn't call him by that full name.

Tom: Yeah, probably didn't.

Will: But he would generally explain that so—we didn't call him by that name.

Tom: But Brother Will, how did you start being the priest for country music singers, writers, and so forth. You were a priest and you knew them?

Will: Well, when I came here from Ole Miss and we didn't have money. I think we had a little house down on 16th Avenue and all of a sudden that's where a lot of the country music people landed. They came to town the way I did. They didn't have anything and you would either get an apartment or office down there on 16th Avenue and that's how I met them. Bob Ferguson—do you know what he wrote?

Bob: He sounds familiar.

Will: He had one very famous song, "On the Wings of a Dove."

Bob: Oh yeah, great song.

Will: He wrote that and said why do any more?

Bob: Everybody and his brother recorded that song.

Tom: Is he one of the guys you met there on 16th Avenue?

Will: Yeah, 16th Avenue. And Kristofferson.

Tom: Tell me a little about Kristofferson and how you met him and so forth.

Will: Kristofferson came by and I wish to hell I could find my stuff about him. But he came by one time and said to my secretary, "I read in *Life* magazine, where there is a guy who marches with the Ku Klux Klan and loves MLK. What the hell—who is that—what's going on?"

And my secretary said, "Well go right down that hall and you can talk to him. That's who it is." And he said, "What's his name?"

She said, "You can ask him his name, he knows."

He said, "Well, this guy's name is Campbell."

She said, "Go back there and talk to him." So he and one of the Kershaw boys, not Doug but the other, came to my office.

Bob: Sammy.

Will: There were three of those boys.

Bob: One of them was named Sammy.

Will: Yeah, but that was the three. Doug Kershaw—anyway, they came back there and started talking and he said "Who the hell are you?" and I said, "Nobody. My name is Will Campbell. What's your name?" He said, "Well, you never heard of me but I'm going to be a great songwriter." "Well, I probably am too," I told him.

Bob: Well, you both were as it turned out.

Will: So, about that time a woman came in from next door and she was crying and saying he's dead, he's dead, he's dead, and we thought she was talking about her husband. The Kershaw boy said, "Reverend, I think you better go talk to her. She needs somebody to talk to."

As it turned out, she was Kathy Greggory and her husband, Bobby Greggory, wrote one famous country song, "Here Rattler Here." The deceased was a dog in a little casket. Yes, we conducted a funeral and they all sang "Here Rattler Here." Sometimes people will just keep adding to these stories.

Bob: I'm sure none of this is fiction.

Will: I had a divinity student at Vanderbilt and loyal employee working for me at the time. He claims he remembers everything except the funeral. But he said "I'm prepared to say that everything, every word in this book Will Campbell's written is true and I was right there when it happened."

Tom: Okay, as long as he was a real divinity student and a loyal employee—that covers it.

Bob: Well, he was probably overcome with grief and had to just say he remembered it all.

Tom: Was there a dead man anywhere?

Will: We still hadn't been next door checking this out but Kris wrote a song about it.

Tom: Did Kristofferson ask for your advice about staying in that business or what?

Will: No, he knew where he was going and where he had been.

Tom: How long did you know him?

Will: At that time?

Tom: Yes

Will: Probably a year—and he got to know Fred Foster who was a big record song producer and that's when he started peddling his songs.

Tom: Took off from there?

Will: Yeah, went on up pretty fast. Then he disappeared and went to Hollywood.

Tom: When did you meet Willie [Nelson]?

Will: I met Willie through Waylon when I was riding with Waylon, and I have a chapter in this book about Willie. I could print one up for you. Brenda came through that door one day and said one of us had to get out and get a real job, and I told Waylon I needed a job and he said, well, you've got it.

Tom: Were you riding with Waylon when you all came down to Jackson?

Will: No, that was just a pleasure trip and I guess that was the last trip I made with Waylon. He was sick already. He wanted to meet the high sheriff. And I said I know the sheriff. What is his name?

Bob: McMillin.

Will: Yeah, I had known him; I forgot how I first knew him.

Tom: Yeah. I was just asking when was the first time you met Willie and all them. Tom T. Hall, of course, is another story. When did you meet Tom T.?

Will: Let's see, there was a book that Tom liked and the guy who wrote it was in town.

Tom: Was Tom pretty famous when you met him?

Will: Yes.

Tom: What do you think about country music these days?

Will: It's not what it used to be

Tom: How would you describe it now?

Will: It's more like pop—I can't tell anymore what country is and what's pop. I get mixed up. I'm trying to find my little book.

Bob: The book you're working on? Now here's something. It says "I met Porter Wagoner." Is that part of what you have there?

Will: Yeah, that's part of it.

Bob: Yeah, this is going to be it with these clips on it I bet.

Will: Maybe.

Bob: How did you meet Dwight Yoakam?

Will: I met him at Earl Scruggs's wife's funeral.

Bob: Dwight Yoakam is from Kentucky as is Tom T, I just wondered.

Will: No, I don't think they were friends. T. doesn't know him; he doesn't have many friends in country. He really doesn't like them. He says they don't have anything to talk about. They're not as smart as he is, he thinks, which is true.

Tom: Well, who is as smart as Tom T. except Brother Will and the Judge?

Bob: I wouldn't be surprised to learn that most modern country musicians are not as smart as Tom T.

Will: It is so.

Bob: Is Porter Wagoner still living?

Will: No, he died about a year ago, I guess. I didn't know Porter very well, but I knew him.

Bob: What about Dolly [Parton]? Did you cross her path—did you wish too?

Will: I wished to. A friend of mine—I call her my Chattanooga doctor—she was on the phone when we walked in here. She keeps bullying me. She's from up there where Dolly is from and she said you need to have Dolly in this book you are writing. I said, but I didn't know Dolly. She said, well I'll introduce her and then you will know her. I admire her, I think she's brilliant.

Bob: Obviously she's pulled herself up by her own bootstrap from the stories I've heard.

Will: Billy Bob Thornton—that's the guy's name I was trying to recall.

Bob: Billy Bob Thornton.

Will: And they were both in that movie *Sling Blade*. Have you seen that?

Bob: I like it so much I bought the videotape.

Will: It's a heck of a movie.

Bob: It's a piece of literature. I really like that movie.

Will: I happened to see them both and I liked the both of them. I asked them what they thought of our war. They said, "Do we have to talk about that. This guy, you know, you referred to him as our president—he's not my president." I said, God knows he's not mine either. No wonder you're such a great actor, you're so bright. Dwight Yoakam and Jerry Clower.

Bob: Clower was your cousin wasn't he? Jerry Clower—you all were kin, weren't you?

Will: He married my first cousin.

Bob: Oh.

Will: He didn't like us after he became rich and famous.

Bob: Did he have a problem with your civil rights work?

Will: Yeah, but then he became a great champion.

Bob: Didn't you tell me he wrote you a bad letter once?

Will: That letter is stacked I'm sure. I gave the Campbell papers to Southern. They came over here and got them. I didn't keep anything. The guy said what's in that filing cabinet? I said just junk. He said can I have the junk. So he loaded the junk. Somebody was doing some research there and she told me she found a letter from Jerry Clower. She knew about our relation, and she said I don't think you want that letter in print. I told them when they took it that everything in that filing cabinet belonged to them. She said well, you check that out and if there's anything in there you want, you get it out. But I never really did and that's the way he felt at that time. So I decided to leave it in there.

Bob: Was he chastising you?

Will: Oh, lord yes.

Bob: So you remember, I'm sure, the archivist down at USM, Bobs Tusa. Was she the archivist when you gave your papers?

Will: No, I think she left there not long after that. Don't they have your papers of a sort?

Bob: No, they don't. They got the William Harris Hardy papers which I arranged for them. I knew some of his descendants and I got them together with Dr. Tusa. Dr. Tusa asked for my papers and I said I am not anybody. I don't have any papers. She said well if you get any I want them. But I guess I've letters from you and other people who are respected in their field. So maybe I'll have some papers one day.

Will: You've got more respect than that. We're just sitting around here telling lies.

Tom: Well, what do y'all think about winding up?

Bob: Probably so.

Will: I'm just getting started. What I am looking for now?

Bob: You never said what you're looking for, you were just looking I think.

Tom: I think so too. For the record you are looking at notes and drafts on your next book.

Bob: That's the snapshots of people he encountered while on 16th Avenue in Nashville and environs.

Tom: You wouldn't want us to use that would you Will?

Will: What?

Tom: The stuff you're working on. I hope you are going to write that.

Will: Well, not as is. You may get some ideas from it. Well, I'd have to type it up. Maybe one day I will, maybe I won't.

Bob: Well, either do it or get it done. That would be interesting.

Tom: Yeah, it will be.

Will: Well, it answers a lot of questions. Like you asking about Kristofferson—that's how we met and we still have a good time anytime we're together.

Bob: When was the last time you heard from him?

Will: I guess the last time he sang in Nashville I was there and he sang that song he sings about the two little Okie boys asking how much is the candies in the window and the clerk says two for a penny and he said we just have a penny. The little kids left and there were these truck drivers over there. They said the candy is two for a penny and she said what's it to you. Later when the truckers were leaving, they didn't pay enough on the tip and the clerk pointed it out. They said what's that to you?

Bob: Yeah, I remember that song,

Tom: That was kind of a truck driver story. Kris is deep. His songs are brilliant. And you sure had a lot of influence on a lot of people. I am going to keep you and all my Episcopal preachers. You're not only a preacher but a writer of rare books, and many other things. Did I say Christian? I told Jim Whitehead that he argued with you because he never understood that you really do like Jesus and believe what he said. You didn't just parrot Jesus's words. Will, you would back that Dude against anyone else.

Will: I know what that is.

Bob: It depends on who you ask.

Will: "Okie from Muskogee"?

Bob: That's an old Merle Haggard song.

Will: I don't know Haggard.

Bob: He puts on a good show.

Will: Yeah, he's good.

Bob: Tom and I saw him and Bob Dylan in Jackson a few years ago. Did Bob Dylan ever come through here?

Will: I don't know. I never met him.

Bob: Seems like he would be an interesting—well, I'd be scared to initiate a conversation.

Will: I don't know.

Bob: Well, Tom.

Tom: Yes sir?

Bob: Have you exhausted your questions?

Tom: Yeah, I think so. We do appreciate it, Will. Thanks for the hospitality.

Key Resources

Books

Connelly, Thomas. *Will Campbell and the Soul of the South*. New York: Continuum, 1982.

Egerton, John. *A Mind to Stay Here: Profiles from the South*. New York: Macmillan, 1970, 15–31.

Gaillard, Frye. "The Scandalous Gospel of Will Campbell." In *Race, Rock, and Religion: Profiles from a Southern Journalist*. Charlotte: East Woods Press, 1982, 46.

Hawkins, Merrill M., Jr. *Will Campbell: Radical Prophet of the South*. Macon, Ga.: Mercer University Press, 1997, 153–84.

Wright, Lawrence. *Saints and Sinners: Walker Railey, Jimmy Swaggart, Madalyn Murray O'Hair, Anton LaVey, Will Campbell, Matthew Fox*. New York: Alfred A. Knopf. 1993, 157–202.

Articles

Carder, Kenneth. "Bubba to a Gadfly—Remembering Will D. Campbell." *Faith and Leadership*, June 18, 2013. http://www.faithandleadership.com/content/ken-carder-bubba-gadfly-remembering-will-d-campbell.

Collum, Danny Duncan, "The Passing of a Prophet." *Sojourners*, September–October 2013. https://sojo.net/magazine/september-october-2013/passing-prophet.

Egerton, John. "Rev. Will D. Campbell, Southern Racial Reconciler." *Southern Spaces*, June 6, 2013. http://southernspaces.org/2013/reverend-will-d-campbell-southern-racial-reconciler#section1.

Ford, Jennifer. "Will Campbell and Christ's Ambassadors: Selections from the *Katallagete*/James Y. Holloway Collection, Special Collections, University of Mississippi." *Journal of Southern Religion*, August 2000. http://jsr.fsu.edu/ford.htm.

Frady, Marshall. "Fighter for Forgotten Men." *Life*, June 16, 1972.

Gaillard, Frye. "Appreciating Will Campbell, Preacher to the Damned." *The Progressive*, April 2014.

George, Timothy. "Southern Baptist Theology: Whence and Whither?" *Founders Journal* 19/20 (1995): 29–30. http://founders.org/fj19/southern-baptist-theology-whence-and-whither/.

George, Timothy. "Southern Baptist Theology: Will Campbell, Bootleg Baptist." *First Things Journal*, June 17, 2013. http://www.firstthings.com/web-exclusives/2013/06/will-d-campbell-bootleg-baptist.

Grooms, Bart. "The Preacher Who Didn't Like Church." *black & white*, August 5, 2000.

Houston, Benjamin. "'The Aquinas of the Rednecks': Reconciliation, the Southern Character, and the Bootleg Ministry of Will D. Campbell." *The Sixties: A Journal of History, Politics and Culture* 4, no. 2, 135–50. http://dx.doi.org/10.1080/17541328.2011.625196.

Johnson, Rheta G. "Scholarly Mississippi Conference Depicts Elvis Presley Not as Star but Victim." *Atlanta Journal Constitution*, September 14, 1995.

Joyce, Adam. "What I Learned from Will Campbell." The Washington Institute for Faith, Vocation, and Culture, June 10, 2013. http://www.washingtonist.org/5014/what-i-learned-from-will-campbell/.

Kennedy, Thomas. "Gimme That Old Time Religion: John Crowe Ransom and Will D. Campbell as Critics of American Religion." *Border States: Journal of Tennessee-Kentucky American Studies Association* 7 (March 1989).

Leonard, Bill. "The Freedom of Will." *Associated Baptist Press*, June 4, 2013. http://www.abpnews.com/opinion/item/8554-the-freedom-of-will.

Sweat, Joseph. "Nothing Sacred." *Nashville Scene*, December 1, 2005. www.nashvillescene.com/nashville/nothing-sacred/Content/oid.

Manuscript Collection

Campbell (Will D.) Papers. University of Southern Mississippi, McCain Library and Archives. www.lib.usm.edu/legacy/archives/m341text.htm.

Index

CPSIA information can be obtained
at www.ICGtesting.com
Printed in the USA
FFOW03n1323180418
46307497-47835FF